THE WESLEYAN-ARMINIAN DOCTRINE of ELECTION

Vic Reasoner

2120 Culverson Ave
Evansville, IN 47714-4811

© 2025 Victor Paul Reasoner
ISBN 979-8-9937696-9-1
Library of Congress Control Number:
2025950985

Eleição Condicional — Coleção Arminianismo was first published in Brazil, in Portuguese, in 2021. It was translated by Dr. Vinicius Couto from this mss.

TABLE of CONTENTS

Introduction 4
The Vocabulary of Predestination 6
Election in Romans 8 28
Election in Romans 9 59
Election in Ephesians 71
Election in 1-2 Peter 75
A Theology of Election 96
Bibliography 108

INTRODUCTION

God is sovereign. But has he predestined everything which happens? Is my salvation based upon his unconditional election? Withing the evangelical community, Arminians and Calvinists have given different answers to these questions. Calvin and Arminius are major theologians in historical Christianity. John Calvin was a leading Reformation theologian of the sixteenth century who built on the theology of Augustine who lived in the fourth and fifth centuries. Jacob Arminius came later, living in the sixteenth and seventeenth centuries. John Wesley adopted an Arminian interpretation to these questions in the eighteenth century. I am writing to present the Wesleyan-Arminian answer, but I will quote leading Calvinists so that you can evaluate their answer out for yourselves and see the contrast in views.

The Calvinist and the Arminian may start with the same *sola Scriptura* premise, exegete the Scripture utilizing the same grammatical-historical hermeneutic, and arrive at opposite conclusions on some topics. When such polar opposite conclusions are drawn from the same source, using the same methodology, the solution is not to consign the other side to hell but rather for both sides to retrace their steps and see which side has been more consistent in the development of their systematic theology.

We are not here by accident. God has a purpose for our lives. That much is agreed upon by both sides. The words *foreknowledge, predestination, calling, election, will,* and *purpose* refer to the plan of God for us. We must have a biblical understanding of these basic terms if we are to arrive at biblical conclusions. Let's begin by defining the basic theological terms.

THE VOCABULARY OF PREDESTINATION

Foreknowledge (πρόγνωσις - *prognosis*) means to know beforehand. As a verb it occurs five times: Romans 8:29, 11:2; 1 Peter 1:20. Two of the references, Acts 26:5 and 2 Peter 3:17 refer to prior knowledge known by humans. As a noun foreknowledge is used twice: Acts 2:23 and 1 Peter 1:2. We have carried the noun form over to English and speak of a *prognosis* as a prediction based on prior knowledge.

In the fourth century Ambrosiaster wrote,

> God foresees everything and knew who would believe in Christ. . . . Therefore those whom God is said to call are the ones who persevere in the faith. These are the people whom he chose before the foundation of the world in Christ.[1]

We have difficulty understanding how God could foreknow the outcome of contingent events. Thomas Oden wrote, "God not only grasps and understands what actually will happen, but also what could happen under varied possible contingencies."[2]

Recently, some radical Arminians have taught process

---

[1] Ambrosiaster, *ACT*, 36.

[2] Oden, *The Living God*, 72.

theology — that God is evolving with us in time and therefore does not know the future in absolute detail. They teach that man's future free choices cannot be foreknown by God; if they were then they would not longer be free.

Therefore, God's foreknowledge is limited and he learns new things as people make choices. Yet the Scripture claims foreknowledge as a part of God's omniscience and God demonstrates his foreknowledge through fulfilled Bible prophecy and so this answer raises more questions than it can answer.

Jacob Arminius taught that God does indeed foreknow our free acts but that his foreknowing them does not cause or necessitate them.[3] W. B. Pope explained,

> The Predestinarian view of the Christian Faith has required the entire removal of any distinction between foreknowledge and foreordination. If from eternity God has foreknown all that is to be, it seems hard to separate this from an immutable destiny appointed for all things. Whatever is foreknown truly must come to pass as it is foreknown But — granting the unsearchable mystery that to the Divine mind all processes are already results — we may be bold to say that logically there is no ground for such a conclusion. It is not the Divine foreknowledge that conditions what takes place but what takes place conditions the Divine foreknowledge. . . . Predestination must have its rights: all that God wills to do is foredetermined. But what human freedom accomplished God can only foreknow: otherwise freedom

---

[3] Arminius, *Works*, 2:368.

is no longer freedom.[4]

The most definitive Wesleyan-Arminian statement was made by Richard Watson, the first systematic theologian of early Methodism. He stated that free actions foreknown do not cease to be contingent. They are known certainly, but are not necessary. The certainty of a free action does not result from the knowledge of it, but from the voluntary determination of the human will. It alters not the case in the least to say that the voluntary action might have been otherwise. Had it been otherwise, the knowledge of it would have been otherwise. The foreknowledge of God then has no influence upon either the freedom or the certainty of actions.[5]

According to Romans 8:29, "whom he did foreknow he also did predestinate." Foreknowing all who would accept Christ, God predestinated these to salvation.

Predestination (προορίζω - *pro* + *horizo*) occurs in Acts 4:28; Romans 8:29-30; 1 Corinthians 2:7; Ephesians 1:5 and 11. This word means to determine or mark out beforehand. It designates the purpose of God. The horizon marks out the boundary of vision. Predestination is like the boundaries marked out on a ball field. We must live within the boundaries God has designated.

However, God does not predetermine that a certain number of people will be saved. Rather, he predetermines the plan of salvation. Hermann Cremer pointed out, the question is not "*who* are the objects of this predestination, but *what* they are

---

[4]Pope, *Compendium*, 1:317.

[5]Watson, *Theological Institutes*, 1:86-88; 375-398.

predestined to."[6] The plan of salvation is certain, but not the unconditional security of the elect.

Yet John Frame, a leading contemporary Calvinist, declared that everything begins in God's eternal plan.

> Hard as it is to understand, that must also be the case with sin. Sin is one of the 'all things' that God works 'according to the counsel of his will,' as Paul says in Ephesians 1:11. . . . Sin did not take God by surprise. God planned it, and if he planned it, he certainly planned it for a holy and good purpose.[7]

Frame concluded that "we should not assume, as Arminians do, that divine permission is anything less than sovereign ordination. . . . Permission, then, is a form of ordination, a form of causation."[8] Here Frame echoes Jonathan Edwards, who taught that God "disposes" all events in such a way that sin "will most certainly and infallibly follow," but he does so for his own "wise, holy and most excellent ends and purposes."[9] R. C. Sproul, Jr. wrote, "Yes, God created sin."[10]

James Daane explained the Calvinistic position, that all things are ontologically necessary, flowing from the essence of God. Therefore, God is fully responsible for sin and evil.[11] And if God predestined sin, then it would cease to be sin and

---

[6]Cremer, *Lexicon*, 462.

[7]Frame, *Salvation Belongs to the Lord*, 102.

[8]Frame, *The Doctrine of God*, 178.

[9]Edwards, *Freedom of the Will*, 399.

[10]Sproul, *Almighty Over All*, 54.

[11]Daane, *Freedom of God*, 79-80.

God would no longer be the ultimate good. However, in order to allow humanity a bonafide freedom of choice, there is a sense in which God permitted sin. But Calvin denied that there is any "mere permission" God.[12] Calvin also wrote that Adam's fall was "not without God's knowledge and ordination."[13]

However, *in love* can modify *chosen, holy and unblemished*, or *by predestinating* in Ephesians 1:5. The NIV adopts the third option, making a new sentence begin with the words, "In love he predestined." This would mean that God's motivation in predestination is his love. A. Skevington Wood observed,

> That has the effect of emphasizing the loving nature of predestination. Any interpretation of this mysterious doctrine that detracts from the love of God is rightly suspect.[14]

But Augustine had written that the number of the predestined is certain, and can neither be increased nor diminished.[15] He taught

> God predestined some to eternal life, not by a foresight of their merit, but of his own good pleasure to show his mercy; but the rest in the same mass, he has reprobated from the celestial kingdom, not by a foresight of their personal demerit, but for his own

---

[12] Calvin, *Concerning the Eternal Predestination of God*, 176.

[13] Calvin, *Concerning the Eternal Predestination of God*, 121.

[14] Wood, *Expositor's Bible Commentary*, 11:24.

[15] Augustine, "On Rebuke and Grace," Chapter 39. *NPNF*1 5:487.

good pleasure, to show his divine righteousness in leaving them in the perdition to which they were justly adjudged.[16]

This conclusion becomes the starting point of John Calvin. According to Calvin, the efficient cause of our salvation is the good pleasure of God's will. The material cause is Jesus Christ. The formal cause is the preaching of the gospel. Preaching is the instrument of faith and the Holy Spirit makes preaching efficacious to the elect. The final cause is the praise of the glory of his grace. Calvin's concern is that the whole glory of our salvation be ascribed undividedly to God alone.[17]

While Calvin is right to exclude all human merit, his doctrine of predestination ultimately fails to explain how the love of God predestined some for reprobation before they were ever created. In Scripture the idea of reprobation is never explicitly contrasted with election.[18] Therefore, when God elects there is no indication that there is a dislike for the persons not chosen. Yet Leroy Forlines has estimated that 80% of all the commentaries on Romans advocate unconditional election.[19]

Charles Hodge is such an example. He declared that the elect are not in Christ through their voluntary union with Christ by faith. On the contrary their election is the ground of

---

[16]cited by Sutcliffe, *Commentary*, 2:734-735. On double predestination, see Augustine, *NPNF*1 5.xlvii; 361; see also Letter 190 to Optatus.

[17]Calvin, *Commentary*, 21:200-208.

[18]Schrenk, "ἐκλέγομαι," *TDNT*, 4:175.

[19]Forlines, *Classical Arminianism*, 97-98.

their voluntary union.[20]

Arminians have no problem with the concept that God predestines *events*, but the question is whether he predestines some *individuals* to salvation. This is called unconditional election. Certainly God elects some individuals to perform particular ministries and certainly some nations are chosen to special religious privilege — like the Jews. But does God arbitrarily select some individuals to salvation and pass over others? The main Scriptures used to support this doctrine are:

Genesis 45:5-8	Acts 16:14-15
Exodus 33:19	Romans 8:28
Psalm 115:3	Romans 9:11-25
Jeremiah 1:5	Romans 11:2-32
Luke 1:15	Galatians 1:15
John 1:12	Ephesians 1:4, 11
John 15:16	2 Thessalonians 2:13
Acts 2:23; 4:28	2 Timothy 1:9
Acts 13:48	

While this list looks decisive, each passage must be exegeted and not simply read with Calvinistic presuppositions. In many instances their argument is an argument from silence.

Wesley's conditional view of election was expressed in the words of Mark 16:16. In *Predestination Calmly Considered*, cites twenty-two passages which emphasize human responsibility, thirteen passages which promise that God is willing to save all men, and eleven passages which proclaim

---

[20]Hodge, *Commentary*, 31.

that Christ dies for all men.[21] Wesley said, he that believes is elected to salvation if he endures to the end and the believer is predestined to walk in holiness. That defines true Gospel predestination.[22] Wesley explained that with regard to unconditional election,

> I believe that God, before the foundation of the world did *unconditionally elect* certain persons to do certain works, as Paul to preach the gospel;
> That he has *unconditionally elected* some nations to receive peculiar privileges, the Jewish nation in particular;
> That he has *unconditionally elected* some nations to hear the gospel; as England and Scotland now, and many others in past ages;
> That he has *unconditionally elected* some persons to may peculiar advantages, both with regard to temporal and spiritual things;
> And I do not deny (though I cannot prove it is so), That he has *unconditionally elected* some persons, thence eminently styled, the elect, to eternal glory.
> But I cannot believe,
> That all those who are *not* thus *elected* to glory *must* perish everlastingly; or
> That there is one soul on earth who had not nor ever had a *possibility* of escaping eternal damnation.[23]

---

[21]Wesley, *BE Works*, 13:261-320.

[22]Wesley, *Notes*, 490.

[23]Wesley, *Journal*, 24 August 1743.

In contrast to Calvinism, H. Orton Wiley wrote that

> true predestination is never apart from the free exercise of the human will. God's predetermined purpose is that all, who of their own free volition accept the divine offer of grace through faith alone, shall be conformed to the image of His Son.[24]

This echoes the words of Jacob Arminius,

> Predestination is the decree of the good pleasure of God in Christ, by which He determined within himself from all eternity to justify believers, to adopt them, and to endow them with eternal life.[25]

Clarke explained that God's fixed purpose was to bestow on the Gentiles the blessing of the adoption of sons by Christ Jesus and without circumcision to admit the Gentiles to all the privileges of his church and people. Clarke declared that before the foundation of the Jewish economy God determined that the Gentiles should be called and admitted into all the privileges of Christ's kingdom. "This is the grand key by which this predestination business is unlocked."[26] Sutcliffe explained,

> The Jew can boast no more of being the chosen, the elect and peculiar people of God. This predestination is, that the gentiles should be fellow-heirs of the

---

[24] Wiley, *Ephesians*, 45-46.

[25] Arminius, *Works*, 2:392.

[26] Clarke, *Commentary*, 6:431-432.

same body, and partakers of the promises of Christ by the gospel, or the effusion of the Spirit on all flesh.[27]

Amos Binney wrote that predestination meant that God had

purposed and fore-appointed that all who believe or trust in Christ should receive the adoption of children. . . . The reason why they were chosen was in their foreseen faith, and not in God's arbitrary choice.[28]

Call. According to Romans 8:29-30, "Those God foreknew he also predestined and those he predestined, he also called." This call is not irresistible since Jesus taught that "many are called, few chosen" (Matt 22:14). Those who accept the call to salvation are the *called*, the called-out ones (ἐκκλησία - *ekklesia*), or the elect. The call is the invitation and the elect are those who accept the call.

The Gospel call is the drawing of the Spirit. Jesus said, "No one can come to me unless the Father who sent me draws him" (John 6:44). Yet all men are drawn (John 12:32). The call is stated in passages such as Isaiah 55 and Matthew 11:28-30. This call involves a proclamation of the Gospel, the genuine offer of salvation based on the condition of faith, and the command to submit to the authority of Christ. The Holy Spirit is the agent and the call comes through the Word of God. While this call is stated in Scripture, the church is also

---

[27]Sutcliffe, *Commentary*, 2:738.

[28]Binney, *People's Commentary*, 517-518.

commissioned to go into all the world and declare the terms of salvation. The Holy Spirit usually draws sinners to Christ through the preaching of the gospel (Rom 10:14).

God's purpose to saving the world is made known to everyone by a proclamation of the free offer of grace. The call must be as universal as the benefit of a universal atonement. Thus, the Spirit's calling is efficacious since he makes all who hear it conscious of their responsibility and capable of obedience. However, it is not irresistible. Those who accept the divine call are the elect. "Election always presupposes the call; but the call does not always issue in election."[29] Jesus explained, "For many are invited, but few are chosen" (Matt 22:14). He warned that the Jews "refuse to come to me to have life" (John 5:40). Like their fathers, they "always resist the Holy Spirit" (Acts 7:51). Judas was one of the elect, yet he forfeited his election (John 6:70). Therefore, we must make our calling and election sure (2 Pet 1:10) by enduring to the end (Matt 24:13).

Calvinism, however, teaches that a general or external call is to be preached universally, but that the call is effectual or inward only in the elect. Robert Haldane concluded that the call in Romans 2:4 was merely an external call "without any saving effect."

> From this it evidently follows that God externally calls many to whom He has not purposed to give the grace of conversion. It also follows that it cannot be said that when God thus externally calls persons on whom it is not His purpose to bestow grace, His object is only to render them inexcusable. For if that were the case, the Apostle would not have spoken of

---

[29]Pope, *Compendium*, 2:345.

the riches of His goodness and forbearance, and long-suffering, — terms which would not be applicable, if, by such a call, it was intended merely to render men inexcusable.[30]

This seems to create a moral dilemma for the conscious Calvinistic evangelist which borders on false advertizing. Louis Berkhof, a Calvinistic theologian, wrote that missionaries cannot

> go out and give their hearers the assurance that Christ died for each one of them and that God intends to save each one; but it does mean that they can bring the joyful tidings that Christ died for sinners, that He invites them to come unto Him, and that He offers salvation to all those who truly repent of their sins and accept him with a living faith.[31]

In other words the evangelist can issue a general call, but it will be irresistible only for those who are elect. This destroys the "good news" of the gospel for the reprobate or non-elect.

Actually this call is not irresistible. Jesus taught that "many are called, but few are chosen" (Matt 22:14). "Therefore, my brothers, be all the more eager to make your calling and election sure. For if you do these things you will never fall" (2 Pet 1:10). Oden explained, "The freedom to hear implies also the freedom not to hear, or to hear and to decline

---

[30]Haldane, *Exposition* , 78-79.

[31]Berkhof, *Systematic Theology*, 463.

the invitation."³²

No one can come to Christ unless the Father draws him (John 6:44). When Christ is preached as the object of our faith, the Holy Spirit drawn all men to Christ (John 12:32). While this is a supernatural tug, the Greek verb ἑλκύω (*helkuo*) does not mean that God irresistibly draws the elect. There is no implication that the drawing is either select or irresistible.

In Luke 14:23 the church is commissioned to persuade sinners to come to God's house. However, the verb ἀναγκάζω (*anagkazo*) cannot imply forcing them against their will.

Romans 2:4-5 teaches that the purpose of God's kindness, tolerance, and patience is to lead the sinner toward repentance. While the context here refers specifically to the Jew, it is obvious that they are not unconditionally elect. It should also be noted that ἄγω, which is translated "lead" does not necessarily imply the idea of force or that grace is irresistible. Charles Hodge objected to the statement, "God leads, but man *may* refuse to be led."³³ But Thomas Summers, an Arminian of that same time period, protested, "Leading implies voluntary following; but Hodge says, God makes willing! Were these wretches made willing? Why will men allow themselves to be so biased by peculiar dogmas."³⁴

The word *also* in Romans 2:14-15 indicts the Gentiles as well. The preliminary grace of God informs their conscience to the extent that they are also without excuse if they resist.

Scripture does not distinguish between a general call and an effectual call. Thomas Coke said "effectual calling" was a

---

³²Oden, *The Transforming Grace of God*, 49.

³³Hodge, *Romans*, 48-49.

³⁴Summers, *Romans*, 17-18.

distinction which theologians have invented, without any warrant from Scripture.[35]

While Calvinism teaches that the call of God is irresistible and the election of God is unconditional, Peter teaches we must confirm both. Then he states a condition. For doing these things, you will by no means ever fall. The implication is that if we do not follow through on our commitment that we will fall.

But what does it mean to fall? 2 Peter 1:11 explains that those who do not fall away will be welcomed into heaven. The implication is that those who do fall away will not be welcomed into heaven.

Calvinists object that God is sovereign and his call cannot be resisted. We affirm the sovereignty of God, but believe that God can choose to limit his power. The call is an invitation, not a conscription.

Calvinism tends to talk about "sovereign grace," but the emphasis is always more on sovereignty than grace. Thus, they champion unconditional election and reprobation, as well as irresistible grace. Wesley argued that "the sovereignty of God is then never to be brought to supersede his justice."[36]

He also replied to Calvinists, "You can bring no Scripture proof that God ever did, or assertion that he ever will, act as *mere sovereign* in eternally condemning any soul that ever was or will be born into the world."[37]

James Daane concluded that in Reformed thought, this concept of the sovereignty of grace, that God is free to be gracious to whom he wills, came to mean that God is free

---

[35] Coke, *Commentary*, 5:92.

[36] Wesley, *BE Works*, 13:277.

[37] Wesley, *BE Works*, 13:294.

from any concern about the plight of the world, free in the sense of being unmoved by any moment within history.[38]

Arminians *also* affirm God's sovereignty, but believe that God has the prerogative of not always exercising that sovereignty. In Matthew 23:37-39, God was willing to save Jerusalem, and by extension all mankind. But Jerusalem had the power to temporarily resist the will of God.

Thus, we have true libertarian freedom of the will. Yet God never surrenders the consequences of our free choices to us. He always has the last word. From the Arminian viewpoint, God is so sovereign he can allow human rebellion, yet that rebellion does not thwart his ultimate purpose. He has predestinated the *consequences* of our free choices. Tozer said a god less than sovereign would not bestow moral freedom upon his subjects. He would be afraid to do so. Yet our freedom does not overrule God's sovereignty.[39] C. S. Lewis made a similar statement, "For to make things which are not Itself, and thus to become, in a sense, capable of being resisted by its own handiwork, is the most astonishing and unimaginable of all feats we attribute to omnipotence."[40]

Election. In Ephesians 1:11 κληρόω (*kleroo*) means to be appointed or chosen by lot; to be destined. This is the only time this form of the verb occurs. Calvin said that election is "the foundation and first cause" of all blessings.[41]

Sometimes commentators refer to Old Testament passages where the tribes of Israel were allocated portions of land

---

[38]Daane, *Freedom of God*, 66-67.

[39]Tozer, *The Knowledge of the Holy*, 118.

[40]Lewis, *The Problem of Pain*, 117.

[41]Calvin, *Commentary*, 21:197.

by casting lots. However, if this illustration is pushed too far, it leads to a conclusion that God's choice was arbitrary. While our election is unmerited, it is not arbitrary but based upon God's love. See Deuteronomy 4:20; 9:29; 32:9.

Its meaning is explained by the next clause — *having been predestined*. There is no significant theological distinction between *predestination* and *election*, except that *predestination* implies a time element by its prefix.

Picirilli observed that Paul neither affirms nor denies a condition for election in v 4. But v 13 teaches that faith is the condition through which the decrees made in eternity are administered and experienced in time.[42] Thus, Arminius concluded,

> The passage in Ephesians 1 presupposes faith before predestination. For no one except a believer is predestined to adoption through Christ. "As many as received Him, to them gave He power to become the sons of God."[43]

As a verb ἐκλέγομαι (*eklegomai*) occurs twenty-two times and always in the middle voice — he chooses us for himself. The only exception might be Luke 9:35 which is either in the middle or passive voice.

Jesus chose Judas, but Judas did not choose to follow Jesus. "Have I not chosen you, the Twelve? Yet one of you is a devil!" (John 6:70). We are to make our calling and election sure, for it we do these things we will never fall (2 Pet 1:10). Wiley declared, "We believe to become the elect; we are not

---

[42] Picirilli, *Grace, Faith, Free Will*, 67-70.

[43] Arminius, *Works*, 3:453.

elected to become believers."⁴⁴ Stated more simply, the believers are the elect. Calvinism, however, would contend that the elect are predestined to believe.

Good Pleasure. The term εὐδοκία (*eudokia*) can refer simply to the goodwill felt toward a person. But where there is no reference made to a person as the subject, it means *purpose*. According to Chrysostom, *good pleasure* means God's antecedent will prior to human choices to do evil. His antecedent will is to save all, but his consequent will is that those who become evil should perish.⁴⁵

Arminius wrote about the incredible magnanimity of God. In God's administration of creation, providence, and redemption, he is governed by the highest good (*summum bonum*). God wills what is good. His agenda is to promote the highest good. For the benefit of the creature, God creates a world in which it is possible freely and rightly to relate to God. He creates a world where it is possible to obey, enjoy, glorify, and love God.

Thus, everything God says is utterly truthful. It is impossible that God would communicate anything other than truth. God's righteousness is utterly sincere and simple. It is unthinkable that a perfectly just God is possessed of any hypocrisy or doublespeak. He is consistent in keeping his promises. He is patient, long-suffering, gentle, merciful, and ready to forgive. There is no distinction between God's secret council and his revealed will.

Arminius felt it was almost unthinkable and nearly blasphemous that God would so providentially order and govern

---

⁴⁴Wiley, *Ephesians*, 38.

⁴⁵Edwards, *ACCS*, 8:112.

the universe that it would, by divine design, result in ultimate destruction and ruin. The justice of God does not permit him to destine to eternal death a rational creature who has never sinned. Yet supralapsarianism holds that before creation God foreordained certain individuals to everlasting life and others to eternal destruction. Unless eternal perdition is somehow defined as good, the supralapsarian position holds that God decreed something for evil. In order to demonstrate his justice and mercy, God would have to do something that is neither just nor merciful. Arminius concluded that alternative systems within Calvinism, such as infralapsarianism, also fail to avoid the conclusion that God is the author of sin. He asked, "Does the Justice of God permit him to destine to eternal death a rational creature who has never sinned? We reply in the negative."[46]

Will. The Greek word θέλμα (*thelma*) occurs in Ephesians 1:5, 9, 11. God's will is based upon his good pleasure or favor (vv 5, 9). Moule described the purpose of his will as his "deliberate beneficent resolve."[47] Wesley said that God's unalterable decree was that he who believes shall be delivered.[48]

W. B. Pope pointed out that when we ascribe a will to God, we cannot maintain a pantheistic concept of God. This concept of God's will forces us to understand God as a person.[49]

While Jesus taught us to pray for God's will to be done

---

[46]Stanglin and McCall, *Jacob Arminius*, 72-79.

[47]Moule, *Studies in Ephesians*, 48.

[48]Wesley, *Notes*, 490.

[49]Pope, *Compendium*, 1:308.

on earth, we cannot conclude that whatever happens on earth is necessarily his will. The text does not say that God has a secret will contrary to his revealed will, as stated in 2 Peter 3:8. Nor does it say that God's will is a mystery. Rather it declares that the *mystery* flows from his will. Since Paul reveals this mystery, God's will is no longer a mystery.

In v 11 an additional word βουλή (*boule*) is used. *Boule* refers to idea of purpose and deliberation — the counsel of his will. This word describes the counsel or plan of God. W. B. Pope explained,

> *The counsel of His own will* is simply the decree of His supreme volition: the βουλή is the expression of the θέλημα; it represents our redemption as the primitive norm or rule according to which God *worketh all things,* rather than as a scheme or expedient itself evolved in the Divine mind. Those passages which are sometimes quoted in the later sense refer to the gradual evolution of the heavenly counsel, the conditions on which personal salvation is suspended and the methods of the Spirit's administration.[50]

Commenting on Ephesians 1:11, Pope explained that θέλημα is the exercise of God's will; βουλή is the determination of that will, and ἐνεργέω is the outworking of his will in his acts.[51]

According to Richard Hooker, it is erroneous to think that there is no reason to God's will except that it is his will.

---

[50]Pope, *Compendium,* 2:91.

[51]Pope, *Compendium,* 1:308.

Salmond elaborated that this word *counsel* implies intelligence and deliberation, not acting arbitrarily.[52] Although God's sovereignty is an accepted truth, it does not necessarily follow that his will is always determinative, compulsory, or coerced. He made mankind in his image and likeness, and part of that image and likeness is true libertarian freedom of choice, which is demonstrated in Luke 7:30, where the Pharisees reject God's purpose (*boule*).

Purpose. In Romans 1:13, 3:25 and Ephesians 1:9 Paul uses a third word with the *pro* prefix which means *before*. The Greek word προτίθεμι (*protithemi*) means to set in place beforehand and refers to the eternal plan or purpose of God. The plan of God centers in Christ. He has been decreed by God as the only savior of men. God has decreed that all who would repent and believe would be received into his favor and God has provided the grace making it possible for all men to turn to Christ and trust in him.

Freedom. We must also deal with two other related terms. Both Calvinism and Arminianism affirm the freedom of the will, but they do not define that freedom alike. How can mankind be free if God is sovereign? The tension between divine sovereignty and human responsibility has been expressed in Calvinism as ***compatiblistic liberty***. This means that man's freedom is compatible with God's determinism. Thus, man was not coerced to sin, even if his original sin was predestined. He is free to comply with God's decisions, but he is not free not to comply.

Thus, man sins because he is a sinner. But Adam was not

---

[52]Salmond, *Expositor's Greek Testament*, 3:264. Salmond quoted Hooker, *Of the Lawes of Ecclesiastical Politie* (1594), 1.2.

created as a sinner. Sin is not part of man's basic essence. Jesus was fully human, although he did not sin. We were not created to be sinners. Sin was the result of a historical event.

In contrast to the language used by Luther and Calvin, Jonathan Edwards presented a rationalistic argument that the will is free, but free only choose evil. Edwards defined *freedom* as the ability to act in accordance with one's own choices. Edwards asserted that a person never "wills anything contrary to his desires, or desires anything contrary to his will."[53] However, since mankind is totally depraved he will never choose anything but evil and sin.

Thus, his concept of freedom is compatible with determinism. But a free will that is compatible with determinism is not free since it is the only choice possible. Edwards' book, along with Luther and Calvin, also advocates the bondage of the will even though he has redefined bondage as freedom.

Wesley responded to Edwards, "There is no blame if they are under a *necessity* of willing. There can be no moral good or evil, unless they have *liberty* as well as *will*."[54]

> Indeed if man were not free, he could not be accountable either for his thoughts, words, or actions. If he were not free, he would not be capable either of reward or punishment. He would be incapable either of virtue or vice, of being either morally good or bad.[55]

Wesley took special delight in citing the language of the

---

[53] Edwards, *Freedom of the Will*, 139.

[54] Wesley, *Thoughts Upon Necessity*, 3.7; *BE Works*, 13:539.

[55] Wesley, "On Predestination," Sermon #58, § 6.

Westminster Confession which stated, "God hath endued the will of man with that natural liberty that is neither forced, nor by an absolute necessity of nature, determined to do good or evil."[56]

The Arminian answer is ***libertarian freedom***. We are not autonomous, but God confers to us our freedom. Our actions are foreknown, but not predetermined by God. Thus, true freedom contains the option of contrary choice.[57] It is significant that John Frame concedes this was the position of the early church until the time Augustine debated Pelagius.[58]

Unless God himself was the author of sin, the problem of evil can only be explained by the angels who fell in the context of libertarian human freedom.[59]

With a proper understanding of these crucial terms, let us now look at a few of the major biblical passages which Calvinists typically appeal to in support of their doctrine of predestination and election.

---

[56]Oden, *John Wesley's Teachings*, 2:180.

[57]Murphree, *Divine Paradoxes*, 74-80.

[58]Frame, *The Doctrine of God*, 138.

[59]See Plantinga, *God, Freedom, and Evil*.

ELECTION IN ROMANS 8

The purpose of God is expressed in the salvation order of Romans 8:29-30. While theologians sometimes speak of God's councils and decrees, Wesley said that the image of God deliberating, consulting, planning, and resolving was based more upon man's mode of operation than upon God's. God, who sees all things at one view, has always possessed the same wisdom, his understanding has always been equally clear, and his wisdom equally infallible.[60] Actually, decrees are never mentioned in Scripture. Arminius developed his own set of decrees in order to accommodate the Calvinistic theological mindset, but Wynkoop argued that Arminianism does not need a theoretical sequence of decrees.[61] But to accommodate the Calvinistic order of degrees, Arminius proposed four decrees:

- God decreed to appoint his Son to Destroy sin through his own death. Christ has been appointed the only Savior of mankind. Thus, Christ is the elect man. Individuals are not elect or reprobate, rather it is the way of salvation which is predestined.
- God decreed that those who would repent and believe

---

[60]Wesley, *Notes,* 384.

[61]Wynkoop, *Foundations of Wesleyan-Arminian Theology,* 101-105.

would be received into his favor.
- God has appointed preliminary grace as the means by which to achieve his purpose.
- God predestines on the basis of his foreknowledge. Thus, God chooses those whom he foreknows will believe.[62]

Joseph Sutcliffe rejected Augustine's careless words that even "sin works for good."[63] Yet Haldane, the classic Calvinist commentator, made a similar claim, "Even the sins of believers work for their good."[64] MacArthur argues that if "all things" is taken at face value, it must include sin. Therefore, he concludes, "God can even cause our own sins to work for our good."[65] John Frame declared, "God planned sin for a holy and good purpose."[66] Edwin Palmer asserted, "It is even Biblical to say that God has foreordained sin. If sin was outside the plan of God, then not a single affair of life would be ruled by God."[67] However, John Fletcher, the Methodist saint and scholar, was indignant that Richard Hill also had said "all sins work for good to the pleasant children."[68]

This claim that sin is part of God's sovereignty borders on new age monism that good and evil are merely human

---

[62]Wynkoop, *Foundations of Wesleyan-Arminian Theology*, 48.

[63]Sutcliffe, *Commentary*, 2:459-460.

[64]Haldane, *Exposition*, 393-394. See also Cranfield, *ICC*, 1:428.

[65]MacArthur, *Romans 1-8*, 480-481. Lloyd-Jones makes the same assertion in *The Final Perseverance of the Saints*, 171.

[66]Frame, *Salvation Belongs to the Lord*, 102.

[67]Palmer, *The Five Points of Calvinism*, 82.

[68]Fletcher, *Works*, 1:214.

illusions. Joseph Benson declared, "sin can, in itself considered, in no case whatever work for good."[69] Benson limited the expression "all things" to providential events. He said that sin can in no case whatever work for good.[70]

Fletcher defined *the called* as those who made their calling sure through faith. "These 'he called,' but not these alone."[71] Many are called, but not all respond to that call. For those who do not respond, the call has been aborted. The called are those who respond to the call. Here Paul indicates that God's calling and election includes Gentiles, as well as Jews.

Joseph Fitzmyer wrote that "the called" must not be restricted to such individual Christians as are predestined. *The called* are those who love him, "all who have responded to the divine call. Human love of God is, then, the result of his initiative, his prevenient call to such love. They are 'called' by the Gospel and its preachers, but even before that by divine prevenience."[72]

God's purpose is to bestow the privilege of sonship upon all, whether Jew or Gentile, who turn to him in true repentance and faith. In Romans 8:28-30 God's realized purpose is traced through the order in which it was accomplished. Each verb in this order of salvation is in the aorist tense, which refers to completed action. God foreknew, foreordained, called, justified, and glorified. Yet Forster and Marston dismiss all this by writing, "There can, of course, be little mean-

---

[69]Benson, *Notes*, 5:74.

[70]Benson, "All Events Blessed to the Righteous," Sermon #139, *Sermons*, 5:57-58.

[71]Fletcher, *Works*, 1:250.

[72]Fitzmyer, *Romans*, 524.

ing to tenses in this process, for the plan was conceived in the mind of God outside of time."[73]

Calvinists since Theodore Beza have depicted these five steps as a golden chain which logically cannot be broken.[74] In 1591 William Perkins wrote *A Golden Chain*, which was dedicated to Theodore Beza and which contained "the order of the causes of Salvation and Damnation." According to R. T. Kendall this book traced the order of salvation from the eternal decrees to the final consummation of all things. The doctrine of double predestination is central. Perkins claimed to defend the Calvinist doctrine that "he hath ordained all men to a certain and everlasting estate: that is, either to salvation or condemnation, for his own glory."[75] In 1600 Christopher Ness wrote,

> The golden chain has so linked the means to the end, and sanctification in order to salvation, that God doth infallibly stir up the elect to the use of the means, as well as bring them to the end by the means.[76]

Handley C. G. Moule declared, "So indissoluble is the chain that the last link is here viewed as an accomplished fact because the first links are so."[77] B. B. Warfield declared, "These five golden links are welded together in one unbreak-

---

[73]Forester and Marston, *God's Strategy in Human History*, 103.

[74]Kendall, *Calvin and English Calvinism*, 55-56; 67.

[75]Kendall, *Calvin and English Calvinism*, 55.

[76]Ness, *The Antidote Against Arminianism*, 58.

[77]Moule, *The Epistle of Paul the Apostle to the Romans*, 157.

able chain, so that all who are set upon in God's gracious distinguishing view are carried on by His grace, step by step, up to the great consummation of that glorification which realizes the promised conformity to the image of God's own Son. It is 'election,' you see, that does all this; for 'whom He fore-knew, …Them He also glorified."[78]

Steele and Thomas interpreted this to mean that before the world began, God knew the exact number whom he predestined to salvation.

> Suppose God foreknew 100 individuals, then He predestined 100, He called 100, He justified 100, and He glorified 100 individuals. None are gained, none are lost. He will bring to salvation each individual whom He set His heart on (loved) before the world began.[79]

Loraine Boettner said "there number is so certain and definite that it cannot be either increased or decreased."[80] Jerry Bridges wrote, "You can rest assured that if you have been justified in the past, you certainly will be glorified in the future."[81] Thus, I have cited classic and contemporary Calvinists who have all adopted this concept of a "golden chain."

However, in 1612 Arminius refuted the logical chain conceived by Perkins. Perkins had claimed that the failure of the believer to persevere means that his faith was only tempo-

---

[78] Quoted by Boettner, *The Reformed Doctrine of Predestination*, 86.

[79] Steele and Thomas, *Romans: An Interpretive Outline*, 70.

[80] Boetnner, *The Reformed Doctrine of Predestination*, 84.

[81] Bridges, "Don't Look Back," 14.

rary and therefore he was not elect. Arminius argued that his own doctrine was effectively no different from Perkins; that the believer can really "fall from that very grace wherewith God embraces him unto life eternal."[82]

According to both Perkins and Arminius, if the believer does not persevere, such a person proves to be non-elect. The difference is that Perkins taught that believers persevere because they were elected. Arminius taught that God elects believers whom he foresees will persevere.

Romans 8:28-30 are not an unbroken chain. God's purpose may be thwarted or aborted at any point. We have a choice and we must continually submit to his purpose (2:5-13; 6:23; 8:12-13; 11:17-22; 14:15; see also 1 Cor 9:27; 10:12; 1 Tim 1:19-20; Heb 6:4-6; 10:26-29, 35-38; 12:14-17). The salvation order is stated from finish to start, as seen from God's perspective. "He speaks as one looking back from the goal, upon the race of faith," wrote Wesley.[83] Thomas Oden wrote, "Here time is being telescoped as if seen by God eternally."[84] Dunn concluded,

> Paul is not inviting reflection on the classic problems of determinism and free will, or thinking in terms of a decree which excludes as well as one which includes. His thought is simply that from the perspective of the end it will be evident that history has been the stage for the unfolding of God's purpose, the purpose of the Creator fulfilling his origi-

---

[82] Arminius, *Works*, 3:460.

[83] Wesley, *Notes*, 384.

[84] Oden, *The Transforming Power of Grace*, 131.

nal intention in creating.⁸⁵

The plan of salvation is certain, but the security of the believer is conditional. It cannot be inferred that all who start will finish, but those who do finish will go through this sequence. Wesley explained that Paul "does not affirm, either here or in any other part of his writings, that precisely the same number of persons are called, justified, and glorified. He does not deny that a believer may fall away and be cut off, between his special calling and his glorification. Neither does he deny that many are called who are never justified. He only affirms that this is the method whereby God leads us, step by step, toward heaven."⁸⁶

With a proper framework of interpretation established, now let us walk through the five steps:

1. God foreknew who would believe (v 29).

Foreknowledge (προγινώσκω - *proginosko*) means to know beforehand.⁸⁷ Robert Haldane, writing as a Calvinist, defined foreknowledge as "the love of God towards those whom He predestinates to be saved through Jesus Christ. All the called of God are foreknown by Him."⁸⁸ This definition presupposes a limited atonement, made only for the elect, whom God loved. Scripture is clear, however, that God loved

---

⁸⁵Dunn, *WBC*, 38A:486.

⁸⁶Wesley, *Notes,* 384.

⁸⁷As a verb, *foreknow* occurs in Acts 26:5; Rom 8:29, 11:2; 1 Peter 1:20; 2 Peter 3:17. As a noun it is found in Acts 2:23 and 1 Peter 1:2.

⁸⁸Haldane, *Exposition*, 397.

the world and gave his Son as a universal atonement. God's foreknowledge is thus limited to the elect by Calvinism.

John Murray, another Calvinist, argued that the text said *"whom* he foreknew." Murray interpreted this to mean "whom he set regard upon" or "whom he knew from eternity with distinguishing affection and delight." Thus Murray concluded *foreknowledge* meant "a sovereign distinguishing love."[89] However, Ernst Käsemann denied that *proginosko* means a pretemporal decree.[90] William Klein concluded that "foreknowledge emphasizes prescience, not selection."[91]

Does God foresee that certain individuals will believe and thus predestinate them to salvation or does he set his heart upon certain individuals and predestinate that they should be called and given faith? Is the individual's faith the *cause* or the *result* of God's predestination? Wesley wrote,

> I now know the sun shines. Yet the sun does not shine because I know it: but I know it because he shines. My knowledge *supposes* the sun to shine, but does not in any wise *cause* it. In like manner God knows that man sins; for he knows all things. Yet we do not sin because he knows it: but he knows it because we sin. And his knowledge *supposes* our sin, but does not in any wise *cause* it.[92]

Guy Duty wrote that "God's foreknowledge is not causal.

---

[89]Murray, *NIC*, 1:316-318.

[90]Käsemann, *Commentary on Romans*, 244, 298.

[91]Klein, *The New Chosen People*, 277.

[92]Wesley, "On Predestination," Sermon #58, § 5.

Fore-ordination is according to foreknowledge."[93] God's foreknowledge is cognitive, not causative.

Martin Luther argued in his book, *The Bondage of the Will*, that it was impossible for God to foreknow the future and for man at the same time to be a free agent. Calvinists tend to blur God's foreknowledge and predestination. For example, Martyn Lloyd-Jones taught, "Predestination is simply a description of the destiny that God has determined and decided upon for the people whom He has foreknown."[94] According to this view, there are no contingent events — God foresees what he decrees. Steele and Thomas wrote that all men are not foreknown by God. Although God knew *about* all men before the world began, he foreknew those whom he predestinated, called, and justified.[95] Barnhouse defined *foreknowledge* as

> an advanced determination to carry though a plan which He has eternally purposed in the counsels of His own will, and which is to be carried through without variation because the Lord brings to pass all that He has thus determined and decreed.[96]

One wonders how Barnhouse would distinguish between his definition of foreknowledge and predestination. The term *foreknowledge* does not carry the added implication of determinism. It simply refers to an aspect of God's omniscience — that he knows beforehand. However, Douglas Moo argued

---

[93]Duty, *If Ye Continue*, 99.

[94]Lloyd-Jones, *The Final Perseverance of the Saints*, 242.

[95]Steele and Thomas, *Romans: An Interpretive Outline*, 132-134.

[96]Barnhouse, *Romans*, 7:160.

that in Romans 11:2 and 1 Peter 1:20 the verb "to foreknow" must mean more than simple foreknowledge.[97] The point in Romans 11:2 is that God knew when he chose the descendants of Abraham to be his chosen people that many of them would not keep covenant. However, God did not predestine their apostasy, although he foreknew it. Ambrosiaster wrote, "Those whom God foreknew would believe in him he also chose to receive the promises."[98]

Marvin Vincent declared that *proginosko* does not mean *foreordain*. "It signifies prescience, not preelection."[99] Yet *The Reformation Study Bible*, containing Calvinistic study notes, declares that foreknowledge "is virtually the equivalent of 'elect.'"[100] This is their presupposition, not necessarily what the Bible is saying.

2. God predestined those he foreknew would believe (v 29).

Predestine (προορίζω - *proorizo*) is made up of πρό - *pro* means before and ὁρίζω - *horizo*, which means to set a boundary. There are three words in v 29 which all begin with this prefix *pro*: foreknew, predestined, and firstborn. Thus, *predestine* means to determine to mark out beforehand, to determine before, foreordain. The verb occurs here (vv 29-30), in Acts 4:28, 1 Corinthians 2:7, and in Ephesians 1:5, 11. Kenneth Grider contends that none of these references pertain

---

[97]Moo, *Romans 1-8*, 577.

[98]Ambrosiaster, *ACT*, 70.

[99]Vincent, *Word Studies in the New Testament*, 3:95.

[100]Sproul, *The Reformation Study Bible*, 1781.

to our eternal destiny.[101] Grider conceded that in v30 *glorified* does refer to destiny, "but the reference is so much disjoined from what is itself said to be predestined that this glorification destiny can hardly be said to be what is itself predestined."[102]

Joseph Wang wrote that all of the six references deal with the plan, the design, the condition of some event, or salvation. It is God's purpose, not the arbitrary determination in advance that certain individuals would be saved, which is predestined.[103]

Except for Augustine (354-430), most of the church fathers were convinced that predestination did not remove human free will. And Augustine himself was not consistent in his statements. Early in his career he explained, "God only predestined those whom he knew would believe and follow the call. Paul refers to them as the 'elect.' For many do not come, even though they have been called, but no one comes who has not been called." In *The City of God* Augustine wrote,

> Therefore we are by no means compelled, either, retaining the prescience of God to take away the freedom of the will, or, retaining the freedom of the will, to deny that He is prescient of future things, which is impious. Be we… faithfully and sincerely confess both.[104]

---

[101]Grider, *A Wesleyan-Holiness Theology*, 249-255.

[102]Grider, "Predestination as Temporal Only," 60.

[103]Wang, *Asbury Bible Commentary*, 991.

[104]Augustine, *City of God*, 5.10. *God*, 5.10. *City of God* was written between AD 413-426.

Yet in his *Predestination of the Saints*, written in AD 428, Augustine declared, "God elected believers in order that they might believe, not because they already believed."[105] Augustine argued that God had decreed before time that only a certain number were elected for salvation. Oden asserted that Augustine's teaching gained a fairly wide consensus in the Western church, but never in the Eastern church. Not only did Calvinism arise within the Protestant church of the West, as a result of Augustinian influence, but within the Roman Catholic Church, the Jansenist movement also held to such doctrines as irresistible grace and limited atonement.[106]

Calvin then carried Augustine's doctrine to the logical conclusion of double predestination. Calvin declared,

> By predestination we mean the eternal decree of God, by which he determined with himself whatever he wished to happen with regard to every man. All are not created on equal terms, but some are preordained to eternal life, others to eternal damnation; and, accordingly, as each has been created for one or other of these ends, we say that he has been predestinated to life or to death.[107]

Loraine Boettner explained that God separates the human race into two portions and ordains one to everlasting life and the other to everlasting death.[108]

---

[105]Bray, *ACC,* 233-237.

[106]Oden, *The Transforming Power of Grace,* 147-149.

[107]Calvin, *Institutes of the Christian Religion,* 3.21.5. See also 3.21.7; 3.33.6.

[108]Boettner, *The Reformed Doctrine of Predestination,* 83.

In this context, however, those who love him are predestined to conformity to the image of Christ. But Francis Schaeffer asserted that "if you have been called by God, if you have believed in Him, you can rest in the assurance that He has predestined you for complete salvation." Schaeffer taught that if we had accepted Jesus as our Savior, we may be sure that God the Father has chosen us. For us to be lost again, God the Father would have to have failed in his choice of us.[109] Schaeffer's entire emphasis is upon what happened in the past; Paul's emphasis is upon what God has purposed *will* happen.

However, according to Ephesians 1:4-5 we are chosen to be holy. Hermann Cremer pointed out, the question is not "*who* are the objects of this predestination, but *what* they are predestined to."[110] Thus, Walter Kaiser explained, "All those who love God are predestined. God has a previously thought-out plan for them. And that plan is to make them like Jesus."[111] This is also what Daniel Steele meant by his assertion that "election is unto sanctification."[112] God predestined that believers would be conformed to the likeness of Christ. Wesley preached that the new birth

> is the change wrought in the whole soul by the almighty Spirit of God ... when it is renewed after the image of God. "Gospel holiness is no less than the image of God stamped upon the heart. It is no other

---

[109]Schaeffer, *The Finished Work of Christ*, 225-226.

[110]Cremer, *Biblico-Theological Lexicon of New Testament Greek*, 462.

[111]Kaiser, *Hard Sayings of the Bible*, 559.

[112]Steele, *Half-Hours*, 105.

than the whole mind which was in Christ Jesus.... Now this holiness can have no existence till we are renewed in the image of our mind. It cannot commence in the soul till that change be wrought, till by the power of the highest overshadowing us we are brought 'from darkness to light, from the power of Satan unto God'; that is till we are born again; which therefore is absolutely necessary in order to holiness.[113]

Watson also said, "The change in regeneration consists in the recovery of the moral image of God upon the heart."[114] While *conformed* contains within it the Greek word *morphe*, which means "form," Paul also uses the word *image* to connect God's purpose in us with his creation of Adam. The image of God, marred in Adam, is stamped upon those who belong to the second Adam.

Yet while the image of Christ is restored when we are born again, it is God's purpose that the image of his Son become more distinct with us and that we become more like him. We are being transformed into his likeness (2 Cor 3:18). The new self is being renewed into the full knowledge of the Creator (Col 3:10). Therefore, Christ is the firstborn. In Jewish culture the firstborn male child had privileged status. Christ is to have the preeminence (Col 1:18). We are adopted children of God, who are to be conformed to Christ so that we are like him.

Beet wrote that when a parent chooses a trade for his underage son, "he predestines the boy. He marks out before-

---

[113]Wesley, "The New Birth," Sermon #45, 2.5 and 3.1.

[114]Watson, *Dictionary*, 815.

hand a path in which he would have him go. This purpose, whether accomplished or not, is predestination."[115]

Foreknowlege and predestination are two distinct and different concepts. Foreknowledge precedes predestination. The biblical order is foreknowledge, then predestination. Yet Haldane says foreknowledge is the choice of persons; predestination the end or purpose of those people for which they are designed.[116] Wright also conflated the two terms in his statement that "God's foreknowledge is simply foreknowledge of his own chosen plan in each person's case."[117]

Thus, Robert Picirilli, a classical Arminian scholar, concludes, "For Calvinists, God knows the future certainly *because he first unconditionally foreordained it*. This in effect makes foreknowledge and predestination synonymous and thus makes foreknowledge an active cause."[118]

Sproul wrote that v 29 has been a very important proof text for those who deny the Calvinistic concept of predestination. He acknowledged the problem of how to answer Arminians who point out that the order of salvation begins with foreknowledge, not predestination. Sproul attempted to answer the dilemma by redefining foreknowledge as the selection of whom God will love.[119] Thus Sproul illustrates what Picirilli was just quoted as concluding. Foreknowledge and predestination are conflated from two concepts into one.

God predestines those whom he foreknows will respond

---

[115] Beet, *Romans*, 244.

[116] Haldane, *Exposition*, 397.

[117] Wright, *No Place for Sovereignty*, 139.

[118] Picirilli, "Foreknowledge, Freedom, and the Future," 266.

[119] Sproul, *The Gospel of God*, 149-152.

to the Gospel. MacArthur objected that if "the Lord simply looked ahead to see who would believe and then chose those particular individuals for salvation," then salvation begins with man's faith. God, then, is obligated to grant salvation and this destroys God's initiative in salvation.[120] But MacArthur is confusing God's foreknowledge with God's call. Through prevenient grace sinners are enabled to respond to God's call. God, in his foreknowledge, knows the final outcome, but does not *cause* it. Thus, salvation is both foreknown and initiated by God, but God initiates the process within those whom he foreknows will ultimately fall away from salvation.

Amos Binney's comments better illuminate the text, "God predetermined to glorify all whom he foreknew as being conformed to the image of his Son, including repentance, faith, and all the conditions requisite for that glorification."[121] Wesley taught concerning predestination that

> It is God's fore-appointing obedient Believers to Salvation, not without, but "according to his Foreknowledge" of all their Works, "from the Foundation of the World." And so likewise he predestinates or fore-appoints all disobedient Unbelievers to Damnation, not without, but "according to his foreknowledge" of all their Works, "from the Foundation of the World."[122]

---

[120]MacArthur, *Romans 1-8*, 494-495.

[121]Binney, *TPC*, 414.

[122]Wesley, *Scripture Doctrine Concerning Predestination, Election, and Reprobation: Extracted from a Late Author*, § 11. This is a 16-page tract published by Wesley in 1741, apparently

Watson argued that the context of v 29 indicates that God foreknows believers who love him. Paul does not refer to an elect unto salvation from the masses of human without respect to their faith. Instead, it is those who have actually embraced the heavenly invitation who are called according to his purpose.

Again, those who are predestined are the same persons who are foreknown and the persons foreknown are true believers. Therefore predestination of which Paul speaks is not the predestination of persons unto faith and obedience, but the predestination of believing and obedient persons unto eternal glory. Samuel Fisk wrote, "Predestination and election do not refer to certain people of the world becoming saved or lost, but they relate to those who are already children of God in respect to certain privileges or positions out ahead; they look forward to what God will work in those who have become His own."[123] Klein said, "Paul's concern in predestination is not *how* people become Christians nor *who* become Christians, but to describe *what* God has foreordained on behalf of those who *are* (or *will be*) Christians."[124] "Predestination does not concern who should, or should not *become* Christians, but rather their destiny *as* Christians," explained Forster and Marston.[125] Believers are elected unto privilege and blessing.

---

extracted from Henry Haggar. It was included in the Benson edition of Wesley's *Works*, 14:382-396, but omitted from the Jackson edition. It also appeared in the *Arminian Magazine* 2 (March 1779) 105-119. This quote is found in the Benson edition, 14:384.

[123]Fisk, *Election and Predestination*, 37.

[124]Klein, *The New Chosen People*, 185; see also p. 279.

[125]Forester and Marston, *God's Strategy in Human History*, 101.

The call to love God is an invitation. Those who obey the call are justified. Those who continue in this grace will be glorified. In other words, the purpose of predestination is not causal, but teleological; it does not determine the future so much as it expresses the goal of grace.

Paul is not speaking of an effectual call, a fictional term invented by those who confine the calling to those who are actually saved. The calling is the invitation, the offer, the publication of the Gospel, not a divine operation in the elect. Summers declared, "Every invitation of the gospel is *effectual*, when it is accepted."[126] Howard Marshall wrote,

> The passage is not a statement about the effectual calling of those whom God foreknew. It is a guarantee that those who have responded to God's call with love (and faith) can be fully assured of his purpose of final glorification for them.[127]

Henry Thiessen wrote that salvation is offered to all. In light of the many passages which offer salvation, "we dare not distinguish between a general call to all and a special call to the elect. Nor need we decide whether God's general call is sincere and His special call is irresistible. God does not mock men. If he offers salvation to all, then He also desires to save all, and to extend the same help to all who choose Him."[128]

Paul here restricts his discussion to believers who have answered the call. But although he speaks of those who are called, they are not the only persons called since our Lord

---

[126]Summers, *Commentary,* 114.

[127]Marshall, *Kept by the Power of God,* 273.

[128]Thiessen, *Introductory Lectures in Systematic Theology,* 350.

declared that "many are called, but few chosen" (Matt 22:14). MacArthur admitted that perhaps most who receive the call described in Matthew 22:14 do not accept it. Yet he declared that in the epistles the same word has a different meaning. According to MacArthur the epistles use the same word to describe effectual calling. MacArthur did not divulge the basis for this conclusion, although it is obviously his theological presuppositions.[129]

Moo asserted that the noun κλῆτοι (*klatoi* - the called) "designates Christians" in a host of passages. While that conclusion is not disputed, the issue is whether that proves they were effectually called. Moo then asserted that "the flurry of occurrences in 1 Cor 7:15-22 reveals that, for Paul, 'to be called by God' is equivalent to 'having become a Christian.'"[130] While the verb καλέω (*kaleo* - to call) occurs nine times in this passage, again, the question begging an answer is whether "the called" were irresistibly drawn or whether they are categorized as "the called" because they responded in faith to God's general call.

Having stated that true believers are foreknown and predestined, Paul introduced the order and method of their salvation to connect that salvation with the work of Christ, that he might be glorified.[131]

Arminius taught that God predestined that believers will receive grace and glory. God predestined the necessity of faith in order to receive salvation. And God also predestined the means to faith: the Word and the Spirit. Through God's grace,

---

[129]MacArthur, *Romans 1-8*, 485. Denney made a similar assertion [*XGT*, 2:652].

[130]Moo, *Romans 1-8*, 567, 576-577.

[131]Watson, *Theological Institutes*, 2:358-361.

we are enabled to believe and those who persevere in faith will receive glorification, the end of God's predestination.[132] This glorification, the future redemption of our bodies, was anticipated in vv 18-25.

3. God called — those who answer become "the called" (v 30).

The Gospel call is universal. Those who respond to God's call (καλέω - *kaleo*) are the called (κλητός - *kletos*; as in v 28; see also 1:6-7). Yet while Christians are both "the called" and "the elect," the two phrases express different concepts. Calling cannot be identified with election.[133] "Called implies a summons or invitation which has been obeyed" wrote William Greathouse.[134] Thus, the call is not based upon the arbitrary election of God in the past, but looks forward. Those whom God foreknows will believe are called *to be* saints (1:7). God has called us to a holy life (2 Tim 1:9).

Yet Calvinism teaches that the call to salvation is based upon God's election; those who were predestined were effectually called. Calvin wrote

> There is the general call, by which God invites all equally to himself through the outward preaching of the word — even those to whom he holds it out as a savor of death, and as the occasion for severer condemnation. The other kind of call is special, which he deigns for the most part to give to the believers

---

[132]Arminius, *Works*,2:392-395.

[133]Klein, *The New Chosen People*, 201-202.

[134]Greathouse, *Beacon Bible Commentary*, 8:191.

alone, while by the inward illumination of his Spirit he causes the preached Word to dwell in their hearts. Yet sometimes he also causes those whom he illumines only for a time to partake of it; then he justly forsakes them on account of their ungratefulness and strikes them with even greater blindness.[135]

While this passage suggests that non-elect could respond to the Gospel and be saved, this would contradict the Calvinistic teaching of God's unchangeable decrees. Jerry Walls concluded that this passage "lends support to Wesley's charge that predestinationism makes God out to be insincere. It is almost as if God were toying with the lost. He gives them a temporary ability to believe, but in the end, it must be withdrawn, for he has chosen them for damnation."[136]

However, the Calvinist theologian Charles Hodge declared

God chooses certain individuals and predestinates them to eternal life. The ground of this choice is his own sovereign pleasure; the end to which the elect are predestinated, is conformity to Jesus Christ, both in character and destiny.... The only evidence of election is effectual calling, that is, the production of holiness. And the only evidence of the genuineness of this call and the certainty of our perseverance, is a patient continuance in well-doing.[137]

---

[135]Calvin, *Institutes of the Christian Religion*, McNeill, ed, 2:974; 1:555-556.

[136]Walls, "Can God Save Anyone He Will?" 166.

[137]Hodge, *Commentary*, 292.

Haldane, likewise, declared,

> In the election of some, and the passing by of others, the wisdom of God is manifest; for by this means He displays both His justice and mercy, — otherwise one of these perfections would not have appeared. If all had been withdrawn from their state of corruption, the justice of God would not have manifested itself in their punishment. If none had been chosen, His mercy would not have been seen. In the salvation of these, God has displayed His grace; and in the punishment of sin in the other, He has discovered His justice and hatred of iniquity.[138]

Therefore, God treats some with justice; others he treats with mercy. MacArthur emphasized strongly that Scripture nowhere teaches reprobation, the doctrine that God chooses unbelievers for condemnation. While reprobation is the logical corollary of God's election of some and passing by of others, MacArthur assured us that "God predestines believers to eternal life, but Scripture *does not* say that He predestines unbelievers to eternal damnation." MacArthur admitted these two truths seem paradoxical to us, but he assured us they are in perfect divine harmony.[139] We can take his word for it and join him to decry any interpretation of the Bible which attempts to harmonize such contradictions. But while some Calvinists will not face the implications of their own system, the final condition of the nonelect remains the same. Boice admitted that it made no difference in the ultimate effect

---

[138] Haldane, *Exposition*, 399.

[139] MacArthur, *Romans 1-8*, 498.

whether reprobation was a passing by or an active ordination.[140] Reprobation is God's decree to be eternally separated from those who are self-determined to refuse the means of grace and remain in sin. Just as in the case of election, God's decree is based upon his foreknowledge.[141] Yet according to 3:26, God, in his mercy, makes salvation available to anyone who have faith and yet maintains total, not partial, justice.

Haldane continued,

> All who are elected are in due time effectually called, and all who are effectually called have been from all eternity elected and ordained to eternal salvation. Effectual calling, then, is the proper and necessary consequence and effect of election, and the means to glorification."[142]

Notice that the word *election* has not yet been used by Paul and does not appear in the book of Romans until v 33. The subject is God's call unto salvation and that call is not based upon election. As it is used in this context, the called are those whom God foreknew would respond. Watson observed that nothing in this passage refers to a set number who are predestined or called. The context refers to true believers.

> Nothing, however, is here said to favor the conclusion, that many others who were *called* by the Gospel, but refused, might not have been justified and glorified as well as they; nothing to distinguish this

---

[140]Boice, *Romans*, 3:1063.

[141]Oden, *The Transforming Power of Grace*, 155.

[142]Haldane, *Exposition*, 402-403.

calling into common and effectual: and the very guilt which those are every where represented as contracting who despised the Gospel calling, shows that they reject a grace which is sufficient, and sincerely intended, to save them.[143]

Mickelsen observed that the pronoun "whom" in v 29 is plural, not singular. From this he argued for corporate election, that God has chosen all who believe in Christ.[144] Corporate election is the view that individuals are elect because they are in the church, not in the church because they are elect. The old ship of Zion is predestined to arrive at heaven's port; it is your responsibility to be on board. This concept will be discussed in chapter 9. Calvinism uniformly holds that it is personal and unconditional. Wesleyan-Arminianism teaches that it is corporate and conditional. Viewed from the perspective of the one — the condition is faith. Yet viewed from the perspective of the many, election is unconditional. Another Arminian option holds that election is personal and conditional.

Roger Olson explained that predestination is simply God's determination or decree to save through Christ all who freely respond to God's offer of free grace by repenting of sin and believing in Christ. "Election is corporate — God's determination of Christ to be the Savior of that group of people who repent and believe; predestination is individual — God's foreknowledge of those who will repent and believe."[145]

However, because those who are called are justified,

---

[143]Watson, *Dictionary*, 194.

[144]Mickelsen, *Wycliffe Bible Commentary*, 1208.

[145]Olson, *Arminian Theology*, 37; 198.

Hodge assumed that this calling is not the mere external call of the Gospel, but the effectual calling.[146] Coke said "effectual calling" was a distinction which divines have invented, without any warrant from Scripture.[147] Yet the Synod of Dort declared,

> He hath chosen a set number of certain men, neither better, nor more worthy than others; but lying in the common misery with others, to salvation in Christ, whom he had also appointed the Mediator and Head of the elect; and the foundation of salvation from all eternity; and so he decreed to give them to him to be saved; and effectually to call, and draw them to a communion with him, by his word and Spirit; or to give them a true faith in him.

While there is no biblical basis for such a claim, Romans 8:28-30 was cited as the proof.[148] *The Reformation Study Bible* declared at v 30,

> The call cannot refer to the outward call of the gospel that many reject. It is an inward call of God that performs what He intends. All who are predestined are called in this way. Predestination includes God's determination that a person will receive such an effectual call.[149]

---

[146]Hodge, *Commentary*, 286

[147]Coke, *Commentary*, 5:92.

[148]Quoted by Watson, *Theological Institutes*, 2:355-356.

[149]Sproul, *The Reformation Study Bible*, 1782.

From that unproven assumption Hodge then drew another, "It is, therefore, included in the very purpose and promise of salvation, that its objects shall be preserved from apostacy [sic] and deadly sins."[150]

4. God justified those who obeyed his call (v 30).

Watson observed that Romans 8 is the conclusion of Paul's discourse on justification by faith, a discourse on the present state of pardon and holiness, as well as the future hope of happiness. It was not Paul's purpose to speak on the doctrine of election and there is nothing in the course of his argument which leads to it. Therefore, v 30 ought not to be considered in isolation from its context. From vv 17-25 Paul has mentioned the assistance and intercession of the Spirit, and the working together of all things for good to them who are the called according to his purpose. These verses connect to the previous section to show that the present sufferings would work together for good in a future state by a glorious resurrection from the dead. The ultimate triumph of grace is God's purpose. All things will work out *because* in God's foreknowledge he has predestined it. Verse 29 is connected to v 28 by the causal particle ὅτι (*hoti* - for or because). Thus, Watson argued that Paul is not teaching that a certain set number of men have been predestined to become Christians, but that Christians who persevere through their present sufferings are predestined to eternal glory. The subjects of v 29 are believers. Since it is believers who love God that are predestined, it must be concluded that it is possible for all who are called to experience the goal of God's predestined plan. If, however, not all are called, but God will punish them ever-

---

[150]Hodge, *Commentary*, 287.

lastingly for not obeying an invitation which he never purposed for them to accept, then the doctrine of reprobation must be acknowledged.[151]

5. God glorified those who continued in his justifying grace (v 30).

Wesley identified vv 29-30 as likely among those things which Peter had in mind when he wrote that Paul had written some things hard to be understood (2 Pet 3:15-16). Wesley denied that the apostle described a chain of causes and effects, but simply showed the method and order in which God works. Colin Williams wrote that Wesley's position, that grace is "free for all and in all," broke "the chain of logical necessity by which the Calvinist doctrine of predestination seems to flow from the doctrine of original sin, by this doctrine of prevenient grace."[152] Clarke observed that everything spoken of in vv 29-30 is conditional. The promises are not made to persons who are elect, but to whomever exhibits the character of holiness.[153] "Having resolved to save," Beet explained,

> He was moved by His infinite wisdom and undeserved favor to select persevering faith as the condition of salvation. And, having chosen this condition, he now uses means to lead men to repentance and faith. So far from our faith being a ground, it is a

---

[151]Watson, *Theological Institutes*, 2:355-361.

[152]Williams, *John Wesley's Theology Today*, 44.

[153]Clarke, *Commentary*, 6:103.

result, of God's predestination.[154]

Since all time is present with God, properly speaking, there is neither foreknowledge nor after-knowledge. Therefore, when God speaks of his own purpose, counsel, plan, or foreknowledge, he uses language which accommodates man's manner of working. God has no need of counsel, of purpose, or of planning his work beforehand. Nor does God's knowledge of all things in any sense causes them.

Predestination is God's decree from everlasting to everlasting that all who believe in the Son of his love shall be conformed to his image, shall be saved from all inward and outward sin. F. F. Bruce said, "Sanctification is glory begun; glory is sanctification completed."[155]

Those whom God foreknows will believe, are called. Implied in this call is their acceptance and justification. Wesley interprets the justified as those whom God has made just, righteous, or sanctified.

The last step is to be glorified and to enter the glory of God's presence. "Who are glorified? None but those who were first sanctified. Who are sanctified? None but those who were first justified? Who are justified? None but those who were first predestinated. Who are predestinated? None but those whom God foreknew as believers." Thus God knows all believers, wills that they should be saved from sin, to that end justifies them, sanctifies and takes them to glory.[156] While some may be concerned that Paul omits sanctification in this sequence, it is certainly implied in the phrase "conformed to

---

[154]Beet, *Commentary*, 245.

[155]Bruce, *TNTC*, 6:178.

[156]This summarizes Wesley's Sermon #58, "On Predestination."

the likeness of his Son."

But the Bible never refers to a set number who are predestined, effectually called, or selected to be saved. God has chosen all who believe in Christ (9:30-32). They are the *elect*. The Gospel call to salvation is not based on election or his pre-selection. Thus, we understand that biblical election is both conditional and corporate. The church is the elect. Individuals are elect because they are in the church, not in the church because they are elect.

In their introduction to Romans 9, Philip and Peter Krey state that ever since Augustine's dispute with Pelagius in the fourth century, the Western church has puzzled over the relationship between divine sovereignty and human freedom. They identify five interpretations concerning election and predestination among the reformers of the sixteenth century. All of these reformers would have considered themselves as the heirs of Augustine and none of them would have been Pelagian. The priority and necessity of grace was nonnegotiable for all of these reformers. Yet some of them were monergistic, meaning that God acts alone, and some were synergistic, meaning that there is a combination of divine and human action. The five interpretations were:

- Double predestination holds that God predestines some to salvation and others to condemnation. John Calvin and Theodore Beza represent this view, as did Martin Luther in his debate with Erasmus.
- Single predestination holds that predestination is only a comfort for believers. Lutheran theologian Philipp Melanchthon held this view
- Freedom of the will holds that man has the freedom to choose eternal salvation or turn away from it. Desiderius Erasmus argued this position

- Conditional predestination holds that predestination is conditioned by God's foreknowledge. This is the view of Jacob Arminius
- The radical reformers held diverse views which tend to cover the first four positions. However, they generally affirmed a greater role for human free will, with some bordering on semi-Pelagianism which holds that while we are fallen, we retain free will and the ability to seek God apart from any special grace.[157]

Paul has already introduced the concept of the one and the many in Romans 5:15-19. This is the key which connects the individual with the group. No man is an island entirely of itself. Sin is personal, but it is also corporate. Salvation is personal, but it is also corporate. The Church is the corporate "new man" of Ephesians 2:15.

The great presumption of the Jews was that they were unconditionally elect. Paul teaches that God's election is corporate, based upon corporate responsibility. But since the whole is the sum of the parts, this also involves personal responsibility. Under the new covenant there has been an expansion of God's elect, due to the unfaithfulness of Israel, and a redefinition of who are the elect.

Nathanael Burwash summarized Paul's doctrine of election:

1. The election was a solidarity, the body of God's people.
2. It was originally constituted and continuously purified and rebuilt on the basis of personal responsibility.
3. This election involved a collective responsibility of the

---

[157]Krey, *Reformation Commentary on Scripture*, 8:xlv-xlviii; 18-19.

entire body as well as an individual responsibility of the units.
4. The Christian dispensation involved, not only a widening, but, on account of the unfaithfulness of the old body, an entire reconstruction of the election.[158]

---

[158]Burwash, *Handbook*, 175.

ELECTION IN ROMANS 9

Thomas Oden wrote that Romans 9-11 was the most crucial passage from which the ideas of double predestination and irresistible grace have been derived.[159] Does Romans 9 teach unconditional election? If we approach Romans 9 with that assumption, then it seems confirmed when we read:

- God chose Isaac and rejected Ishmael
- God chose Jacob and rejected Esau
- God predestined Pharaoh to rebel

Therefore, many have concluded that since God is the potter and we are but clay, he has the right to do anything he wants with us. We are all deserving of damnation. If any are saved, it is only by his sovereign grace. But the Bible never refers to a set number who are predestined and effectually called to be saved. God has chosen all who believe in Christ (Rom 9:30-32). They are the elect. The Gospel call to salvation is not based on a pre-selection. Thus, election is both conditional and corporate. The church is the elect. The basic meaning of the Greek word for church, ἐκκλησία (*ekklesia*) is called out. Abraham was called out and entered into a covenant agreement with God. By the time of Moses the family

---

[159]Oden, *The Transforming Power of Grace*, 132; 142-144; 152; 154; 206-208.

had grown into a nation. The nation of Israel was God's church in the Old Testament. The mystery referred to by Paul was that God intended both Jew and Gentile to be one body (Eph 3:4-6).

Paul has already introduced the concept of the one and the many in Romans 5:15-19. This is the key which connects the individual with the group. No man is an island entirely of himself. Sin is both personal and corporate. Salvation is personal, but also corporate. The church is the corporate "new man" of Ephesians 2:15. Individuals are elect because they are in the church, not in the church because they are elect.

Paul is still dealing with the plan of salvation, but the church in Rome is composed of both Jews and gentiles. While God is just, there was a variation in privilege. Paul taught that God now chooses believing Gentiles to be in the church. Yet this was an offense to the Jews to teach that their superior privilege had ceased.

Martyn Lloyd-Jones, himself a Calvinist, declared that for anyone to exalt predestination as the main theme in this section is almost to be guilty of blasphemy. Paul is still dealing with justification by faith.[160] Yet F. Leroy Forlines found that 80% of the commentaries surveyed on Romans 9 took the position of unconditional election.[161] But I do not think that is what Paul is trying to say. The key to this chapter is that election to service is unconditional, while election to salvation is conditional. Paul is explaining why Israel is not saved, although they were chosen to play a unique role in God's plan. They, too, must be justified by faith, however. Therefore, personal, unconditional election is not Paul's subject.

---

[160]Lloyd-Jones, *God's Sovereign Purpose*, 7.

[161]Forlines, *Romans*, 233.

Seven Reasons why personal, unconditional election is not Paul's subject in Romans 9.

1. The analogy of faith holds that we cannot interpret one passage to contradict the general tenor of Scripture. According to 2 Peter 3:9, God is not wanting anyone to perish, but everyone to come to repentance.

2. The overarching theme of Romans 9 is *not* "Has the word of God failed if most of the Jews are excluded?" Here Calvinism would answer that God has predestined to save only the elect.

Jacob Arminius argued that the real question is — "Has the word of God failed if those Jews who seek salvation by keeping the law, not by faith, are rejected?"[162] And the real answer is that both Jew and gentile are justified by faith (Rom 9:30-32). And so Paul is teaching that election is conditional and that condition is faith. Thus, Arminius restated the older- pre-Augustinian, eastern patristic consensus on grace and freedom.[163]

3. Paul resumes a discussion he began in Romans 3:1-2. There he said that the Jews have greater privilege and he states only one example — they were entrusted with the very words of God. Notice in Romans 9:4-5 Paul continues to enumerate their privileges

- They were adopted as a nation
- The glory cloud; the visible Shekhinah

---

[162] Arminius, *Works*, 3:486.

[163] Oden, *The Transforming Power of Grace*, 152-155.

- the covenants
- the law
- temple worship
- the promises
- the example of the patriarchs
- the Messiah born as a Jew

But these nine blessings do not prove that they are unconditionally elect to salvation. It only means that they were unconditionally chosen to experience greater privilege. As a result, Paul argues that they have greater responsibility. The fact that all these privileges were lost indicates that Israel's election was not unconditional.

If Israel was unconditionally elect, Paul would not write in Romans 11 that they were cut off. Nor would Zechariah declare in 11:10-14 that God would revoke his covenant with Israel. But their apostasy was not final because in Romans 11:26 Paul prophesies that they *will be* saved. Again, he is speaking corporately. But if the covenant with Israel was unconditional, they would have never not been saved.

4. Romans 10:14-17 gives the sequence of salvation. This is the counterpart to Romans 8:29-30. In Romans 8:29-30 we see salvation from God's viewpoint.

- God's foreknowledge
- God's predestination. Notice that the little word *also* implies that foreknowledge is not the same thing as predestination.
- God's call
- God's justification
- God's glorification

While Calvinists often refer to these five steps as an unbroken chain, Wesley held that God speaks as one looking back upon the race of faith from the goal. It cannot be inferred that all who start will finish, but those who finish will experience this process. This interpretation must be correct if we are to reconcile Romans 8:29-30 with Romans 10:14-17.

It is significant that John Piper in his book *The Justification of God* ends his exegetical and theological study in the middle of Romans 9:23. The rest of the chapter, and the one which follows, do not fit his premature conclusions that an essential element of God's glory is his absolute freedom to elect unconditionally and individually those who are arbitrarily the objects of his mercy. Romans 9 ends by teaching that election is corporate (v 24 teaches that he calls gentiles as well as Jews) and based upon faith (vv 30-32).

In Romans 10:14-17 we see human responsibility.

- A preacher must answer the divine call to service and be sent
- His message must be Christ, the object of our faith
- the message must be heard and believed
- sinners must obey by calling on God in faith
- after they are justified they must confess Jesus as Lord

Thus, Romans 10:21 records the forbearance of God. "All day long I held out my hands to a disobedient and obstinate people." This conditional election must be reconciled with the "sovereign grace" which Calvinists claim to find in chapter 9.

5. The election Paul teaches is not only conditional, it is also corporate. John Piper claimed that those who find no individual election in 9:6-13 cannot successfully explain the thread

of Paul's argument as it begins in 9:1-5 and continues through the chapter.[164] But, as I have already observed, Piper abruptly stops at 9:23. Notice the focus of Paul's concern is for his people.

- Paul is concerned about his own race - 9:3
- Paul's desire is for the Israelites - 10:1
- Paul concludes that God has not unconditionally rejected his people - 11:1

But if Paul is teaching corporate election, why does he use personal examples? The individuals represent nations.

1. Isaac and Ishmael – 9:7-9.

They each represent a race: Arab and Jew. Notice in Genesis 21:13, 18 that Hagar was told that Ishmael would *also* become a nation. God is not excluding personal salvation from Ishmael. In fact, God also had a plan for Ishmael in Genesis 17:20. We cannot infer from these verses that Ishmael and his descendants were predestined to reprobation.

2. Jacob and Esau – 9:10-13

According to Genesis 25:23 these twins represent two nations. This passage does not deal with their eternal salvation, but with vocational election. Passages such as Psalm 16:5-6 suggest that God does appoint some of our circumstances — perhaps more than we even recognize.

There is no record that Esau ever personally served Jacob, but according to 2 Samuel 8:14; 1 Chronicles 18:13 the

---

[164]Piper, *The Justification of God*, 40.

Edomites were slaves of Israel. According to Malachi 1:2-3, it was the nation of Edom that was punished some 1600 years after Jacob and Esau lived. Furthermore, it was Esau who first rejected his birthright and covenant blessing. He was not unconditionally reprobate.

As a Calvinist, R. K. McGregor Wright wrote that Romans 9 "looks so distinctively Calvinistic that Arminian exegesis has had a hard time coping with it." The clincher for him is that the destinies of Esau and Jacob were predetermined by God before they were even born or had done anything good or bad.[165] Yet Sanday and Headlam in the *International Critical Commentary* wrote that the absolute election of Jacob "has reference simply to the election of one to higher privileges as head of the chosen race, than the other. It has nothing to do with their eternal salvation."[166]

John Wesley concluded that this passage does not relate on a personal level to either Jacob or Esau. Nor does it address their eternal state or that of their descendants. He concluded, "And yet there is great reason to hope, that Esau (as well as Jacob) is now in Abraham's bosom."[167] His optimism was based on the reconciliation of Jacob and Esau in Genesis 33. However, the hostilities between the two nations continued for centuries. Ultimately, the hope for the Edomites must be based on a universal atonement which included them. Isaiah 19:19-25 suggests that there is room for the families of Ishmael and Esau within Christ's church.

---

[165] Wright, *No Place for Sovereignty*, 123.

[166] Sanday and Headlam, *ICC*, 245.

[167] Wesley, *BE Works*, 13:295.

3. Pharaoh – 9:17-18

Richard Watson pointed out that if Paul's purpose was to teach personal election and reprobation, he would not have used Pharaoh as his third example since Pharaoh was not a descendant of Abraham.[168] Paul quotes Exodus 9:16, "I spared you or kept you alive for this purpose" changing it to read, "I raised you up for this purpose." Paul is saying that God brought Pharaoh onto the stage of human history. The question is whether God created and programed Pharaoh for destruction without any option of contrary choice.

However, Pharaoh personifies the nation of Egypt, much like Caesar personified Rome. The entire nation experienced the ten plagues. When Pharaoh's horses, chariots, and horsemen were drown in the sea, Egypt was destroyed. Thus, this third example is also dealing with corporate election. While Calvinism always treats election as individual, *election*, as described in Scripture is corporate.

According to Exodus 4:21 God in his foreknowledge knew how Pharaoh would respond, but this does not mean that God predestined that response. Again in Exodus 7:3 God tells Moses in advance what will happen. Notice that Pharaoh hardened his own heart eight times before God intervenes. The first time God hardened Pharaoh's heart is in 9:12. God literally strengthened Pharaoh in his rebellion. This was followed by the warning in 9:15-18. God is giving him over to the consequences of his own choices just as Romans 1:24-28 describes. But Pharaoh again hardened his own heart. At some point God quits warning and starts judging by giving us over to what we have chosen. From that point on, God hardened Pharaoh's heart seven more times and Pharaoh hardened

---

[168]Watson, *Theological Institutes*, 2:315-316.

his own heart only once more.

At any stage Pharaoh might have repented and found pardon until God began to harden Pharaoh's heart. Pharaoh made a free choice up to the point that the consequences of his choices begin to take effect.

6. There is an additional argument in Romans 11:16-21 for corporate election in the three illustrations used.

6A. The symbolism of the dough in 11:16. Here Paul alludes to Numbers 15:17-21, where Israel was to offer a cake made from the first ground meal to come from the threshing floor. Wesley explained, "The conversion of a few Jews is an earnest of the conversion of all the rest."[169] Thus, Paul is still describing the restoration of corporate Israel.

6B. The symbolism of the root in 11:16. If Abraham was the root, then the branches whether Jewish or gentile are holy. Again, the metaphor is corporate.

6C. The symbolism of the olive tree in 11:17-21. This metaphor causes great difficulty for Calvinists, who claim that the number of the elect cannot be increased or decreased, since they were decreed by the secret council of God before the foundation of the world. It is also a problem for those who teach the unconditional security of the believer. Wesley concluded, "Therefore, those who are grafted into the good olive tree, the spiritual invisible Church, may nevertheless so fall from God as to perish everlastingly."[170]

But Paul is also teaching continuity. Properly understood,

---

[169] Wesley, *Notes*, 394.

[170] Wesley, *BE Works*, 13:247-248.

this does not teach "replacement theology," that Israel will be replaced by the church, but that the true Israel of God is composed of both Jew and gentile. Again, this is a corporate concept.

This is consistent with Paul's teachings throughout Romans. In Romans 2:28-29 he defines the covenant people of God as those who have experienced and inward circumcision. In Romans 4:10-11, Paul teaches that Abraham was justified by faith prior to his circumcision and that Abraham is the father of *all* who have faith in Jesus Christ. As Paul teaches in Ephesians 2:15, God's eternal purpose is to create one new man out of two. Again, we must recognize that this "man" has a corporate identity.

Calvinists, such as R. C. Sproul, admit that Paul is dealing with Israel. But he argues that since nations are composed of individuals, we cannot avoid individual election.[171] But individual election is not what Paul is addressing here. From a systematic standpoint, Christ is the Chosen One and believers are elect because they are in him.

7. Vocational election is the focus of 9:21. According to 2 Timothy 2:20-21, "In a large house there are articles not only of gold and silver, but also of wood and clay; some are for noble purposes and some for ignoble. If a man [unlike an inanimate object] cleanses himself from the latter, he will be an instrument for noble purposes, made holy, useful to the Master and prepared to do any good work."

The point of this reference is not to suggest the doctrine of supralapsarianism, that God decreed salvation or damnation prior to his creation of mankind. Here again, Calvinism

---

[171]Sproul, *Chosen by God*, 154; *The Gospel of God*, 165; see also Schreiner, *Romans*, 497-498.

imposes its own fatalistic philosophy upon the text.

Calvinism also assumes that vessels of honor and vessels of dishonor correspond to vessels of mercy and vessels of wrath in vv 22-23. They teach that the vessels of mercy are the elect, while the vessels of wrath are the reprobate. But Paul is still teaching corporate election. The vessels of wrath are the Jews and the vessels of mercy are the gentiles. Again, Paul is warning the Jews that they are not unconditionally elect. This is then reinforced by two citations from Hosea 2:23 and 1:10. The gentiles, who were not the people of God, will be recognized by God. The opposite truth is also reinforced by two citations from Isaiah 10:22-23 and 1:9 where they are warned of the danger that only a remnant of Israel will be saved and they could become like Sodom and Gomorrah.

Because this section of Scripture is approached with a priori assumptions which are false, the interpretation of Romans 9-11 is twisted to teach the exact opposite of what Paul meant. Those who twist Romans 9-11 to teach unconditional election tend to affirm biblical inerrancy and the grammatical-historical method of hermeneutics. However, they have not followed their own methodology. I take the Bible just as seriously as they do, and quoted some twenty passages in this lecture which connect with the passage under discussion. Yet a simple inductive study of the passage will not support their conclusions. I believe the greatest privilege given to Israel was the Old Testament, and this is what Paul said in Romans 3:1-2, but it must be interpreted accurately. Israel believed she was unconditionally elect and did not take seriously the warnings from God's prophets.

Thus, Romans 9 teaches that Israel's election was conditional and that condition was faith in the Lord Jesus Christ. Israel was rejected as the elect because they rejected God's

Elect, Jesus Christ. But Romans 11:26 promises that one day all Israel would be saved and grafted back into the tree of God's elect. But Paul also warns the Gentiles that they should not become presumptuous. They, too, are liable to be cut off if they do not keep covenant. Nothing could be more clear. We must persevere in the faith since our election is conditional.

Scripture is the final authority for the church, but we must understand that its promises are conditional and its warnings are real, not hypothetical, as Calvinists tend to regard the warning passages in Hebrews.

ELECTION IN EPHESIANS

Paul gives no guarantee in Ephesians 1:4 that every individual who is presently in Christ will remain in Christ until the *parousia* or judgment day and be declared innocent at that time. Neither predestination nor election in this letter appears to be fixed and final when it comes to individual believers.[172]

The emphasis is not that we chose God, but the wonder that God would take the initiative to choose us. Paul describes salvation from the heavenly perspective. Benson argued that this election was corporate since the choice was made before creation.[173] Longking wrote,

> As constituting a part of God's Church on earth, the Gentile believers, equally with the Jewish, were "chosen" to the possession of "all spiritual blessings." The declaration that this "choice" was "in him" — Christ — shows that the persons thus chosen must be believers, for unbelievers are not "in Christ."[174]

More recently Snodgrass wrote, "Nothing in Ephesians

---

[172]Oropeza, *ANTC*, 2:230.

[173]Benson, *Notes*, 5:302.

[174]Longking, *Notes*, 131-132.

1 focuses on individuals; rather, the text focuses collectively on those who are in Christ."[175]

The verb *chose* (ἐκλέγω - *eklego*) is the only verb in vv 3-14. This verb is aorist middle indicative. The middle voice means he chose us for himself. This indicates personal interest rather than random impersonal choice.[176] Beet explained, "Moved only by pity for lost man, God resolved to save men by means of the good news announced by Christ and to save those who should believe it."[177]

He chose us *that we should be* (present infinitive of purpose). His purpose for us is that we be holy. God is holy. He has always been holy, "but just as he who called you is holy, so be holy in all you do for it is written be holy, because I am holy" (1 Pet 1:15-16). This is what Daniel Steele meant by his assertion that "election is unto sanctification."[178]

Calvin concluded that holiness, purity, and every excellence that is found among men are the fruit of election. "All our holiness and purity of life flow from the election of God." However, Patzia observed that the doctrine of predestination has sometimes led to moral license rather than personal holiness. "Not a few believers have reasoned that since they are 'eternally secure,' their ethical life is no longer of concern to God or to other people."[179] Dennis Kinlaw wrote,

---

[175]Snodgrass, *Ephesians*, 49.

[176]Wallace, *Greek Grammar*, 38, 419-421, 428.

[177]Beet, *Ephesians*, 275.

[178]Steele, *Half-Hours*, 105; see also Oden, *The Transforming Power of Grace*, 141-142.

[179]Patzia, *NIBC*, 153.

Biblical predestination is not God's response to human sin, a divine response to man's fall. God was predestining, according to this passage, before he started creating. The creation was the result of divine predestination. The biblical doctrine of predestination then, according to Paul, is the explanation of what God had in mind when he brought our world and its human beings into existence. Note Paul's use of the reference to God's concept of choice and destiny. His choice was that he would have a world in which he could find a fellowship with persons who would be, as the King James translates it, "holy and without blame before him in love."[180]

According to v 5, God determined to adopt us into his family. Those who believe are the elect. Election is for the purpose of adoption. Longking explained, "These, as believers, then, were chosen to the character and position spoken of before their birth. That to which they were thus 'predestinated' was, 'the adoption of children.'"[181]

George Holden summarized this section,

> That election to which the apostle in this passage (verse 4) refers, is explained in the next verse to be an election or predestination "unto the adoption of children;" which adoption is God's constituting believers to be his family and people, and treating them as sons. This adoption formerly belonged only to the Jews, (Rom 9:4), but now this privilege is

---

[180]Kinlaw, "Ephesians 1: Holy Love."

[181]Longking, *Notes*, 132.

extended through Christ to all believers. Verse 5, then, is explanatory of verse 4, and both connect with verse 3, thus: God hath blessed us believers with all spiritual blessings, (verse 8), since he hath elected us through Christ to the end that we should be holy, (verse 4); and this election consists in having predestinated us to the privilege of being his sons, (verse 5), in order to display the glory of his grace and favor through his beloved Son, (verse 6). Hence the election and predestination spoken of in these verses, relate to God's eternal purpose of bestowing the privilege of adoption to be his sons upon all sincere and obedient believers in Christ; which is adduced as a proof of his having imparted all spiritual blessings to them.[182]

---

[182] Quoted by Longking, *Notes*, 134-135.

ELECTION IN 1-2 PETER

1 Peter 1:20 simply indicates that the plan of salvation was foreknown. God through his foreknowledge knew that we would sin and need a Savior. Christ was the Lamb that was slain from the creation of the world (Rev 13:8). While the foreknowledge that mankind would need a Savior was the basis on which God predestined Christ to be that Savior, this verse cannot be used to prove that God predestines the individual salvation of those whom he elected unconditionally. Methodist commentator Daniel Whedon wrote, "The ark is unconditionally predestined to outride the deluge; but it depends upon our entering and remaining within the ark whether we individually outride the deluge too."[183]

Again, Moo pointed to two occurrences of the noun form, *foreknowledge*. Acts 2:23 stated that the crucifixion was according to the foreknowledge of God. Here, *foreknowledge*, does seems to imply a determination, not simple foreknowledge. But the subject under discussion, again, is not individual predestination to salvation or damnation.

But doesn't 1 Peter 1:2 teach that God chose us according to his foreknowledge? The verb "to choose" (*eklego*) is never used once by Peter. The NIV has it right in v 1; the letter is addressed to God's elect, but then blows it in v 2. The word *chosen* is not in the Greek text. The ESV is more accurate,

---

[183]Whedon, *Commentary*, 3:345.

"To those who are elect exiles of the Dispersion in Pontus, Galatia, Cappadocia, Asia, and Bithynia, according to the foreknowledge of God the Father."

There is just as much precedent to connect the adjective *strangers* with the three prepositional phrases in v 2 as there is to connect the adjective *elect*. Both words are adjectives used as nouns (masculine dative plural). It could just as well be asserted that they were strangers according to the foreknowledge of God, strangers by the sanctification of the Spirit, or strangers unto obedience.

There are four possibilities for the subject of the prepositional phrases of v 2, *according to the foreknowledge of God the Father, through the sanctifying work of the Spirit*. The subject could be Peter the apostle, the elect, the elect strangers in v 1, or grace and peace in v 4.

Edwin Blum wrote that Peter is here announcing some basic themes of his letter that will be later expanded and developed.[184] These themes are not necessarily connected to the doctrine of election. There are four possibilities for the subject of the prepositional phrases of v 2. It could be referring to Peter the apostle, to the elect, to the strangers, or to the grace and peace in v 4. Therefore, Moo fails to conclusively prove that God's foreknowledge of the future state of individuals carries any deterministic meaning.[185]

According to 1 Peter 1:2, God in his foreknowledge saw our sinful plight, and motivated by his holy love, before the

---

[184] Blum, *The Expositor's Bible Commentary*, 12:219.

[185] Moo, *Romans 1-8*, 577. The verb form *foreknow* occurs a total of five times in the NT. Three have been discussed; the other two verses, Acts 26:5 and 2 Peter 3:17, bear no doctrinal significance. The verb form occurs only twice. Both of those references have been discussed.

foundation of the world chose Christ to be the Lamb of God (vv 19-20) who would take away the sin of the world.

Sometimes we are confused by words like *foreknowledge, predestination,* and *election.* Calvinism had given these words a fatalistic definition, implying God in his foreknowledge has chosen that some people are to be saved and some to be lost. Wesley objected that this was no gospel, but along with John Calvin called this teaching a "horrible decree."[186] Wesley was quoting Calvin, *Institutes*, 3.23.7. Calvin, however, believed this was what the Bible taught.

Lorraine Boettner made a significant concession.

> It may occasion some surprise to discover that the doctrine of Predestination was not made a matter of special study until near the end of the fourth century. ... They of course taught that salvation was through Christ; yet they assumed that man had full power to accept or reject the gospel.[187]

It was the later Augustine who introduced the foundation for a Calvinistic understanding of predestination. Yet Vincent of Lérins rejected Augustine's doctrine of predestination because it was not that faith which has been believed everywhere, always, by all. He called it heresy to teach of

> a certain great and special and altogether personal grace of God, so that whosoever pertain to their number, without any labor, without any industry, even though they neither ask, nor seek, nor knock,

---

[186]Wesley, Letter to James Hutton and the Fetter Lane Society, 30 April 1739.

[187]Boettner, *The Reformed Doctrine of Predestination*, 365.

have such a dispensation from God, that, borne up by angel hands, that is, preserved by the protection of angels, it is impossible that should ever dash their feet against a stone, that is, that they should ever be offended.[188]

If Calvinism misunderstands these words, what does the Bible mean by foreknowledge, predestination (although not used by Peter), and election?

Predestination is not connected to election

The question which divides Calvinists and Arminians is whether election is unconditional or conditional. Peter does not address this theological question. Instead, he insists that the elect are predestined to live holy. Wesley explained that those who are the sons of God receive the Spirit of holiness, to walk as Christ also walked.[189] Calvinists also debate whether unconditional election was decreed prior to the fall or afterward. They are divided over speculation regarding the order of the decrees. *Supralapsarianism* holds that there was first election, then creation, then the fall. *Infralapsarianism* argues that creation came first, then the fall, then election. But foreknowledge must be kept distinct from predestination. God foreknew our fall, and this is implied in v 20, but he did not decree our sin.

However, R. C. Sproul insists on what Peter did *not* say.

Predestination must be in relation to that divine

---

[188]Vincent, *Commonitory*, §69; *NPNF* 2. 11:151; 158.

[189]Wesley, *Notes*, 608.

foreknowledge as the basis upon which God knows what He intends to do. . . . God knows the future because He ordains it. He knows His own plan in advance, and He knows it certainly, because He has decreed it.[190]

Adam Clarke argued that if the letter was directed to those who were unconditionally elected to eternal life, no one could have received such a letter, because no one could have been sure of his election in this way until he had arrived in heaven. However, Clarke held to a corporate election which is based upon God's foreknowledge regarding who would believe the gospel.[191]

According to Calvin, election cannot be known without the special revelation of the Spirit. We cannot know whether anyone else is elect, but we should consider those who have been received into the church on the basis of their profession of faith as being elect. Many of them may fall away, but those who are truly elect and effectually called will manifest their election through their sanctification, "for God does not sanctify any but those whom he has previously elected."[192] But this doctrine is little assurance, since Calvin also taught that "so long as we dwell in the prison of the body, we must constantly struggle with the vices of our corrupt nature, and so with our natural disposition."[193]

God, however, predestined the plan of salvation, not

---

[190]Sproul, *1-2 Peter*, 27.

[191]Clarke, *Commentary*, 6:842-843.

[192]Calvin, *Commentary*, 22:24-25.

[193]Calvin, *Institutes*, 3.3.10; 12; 20. See Reasoner, *Holy Living*, 1:390-394.

individual salvation. God has not predestined who will be saved, but he has predestined that those who are born again will be holy. This is exactly what Paul states in 2 Thessalonians 2:13, "God chose you to be saved through the sanctifying work of the Spirit." Note here that "choose" is a verb, but it does not restrict who is chosen, rather it defines what they are chosen to become.

God calls all men everywhere to repent, but that call is not irresistible. "Many are called, but few are chosen" (Matt 20:16; 22:14). Those who respond to God's grace are the elect. In 2 Peter 1:10, the same writer tells us to make our calling and election sure.

The church is comprised of the called out ones. We are called out of the world system and called to be holy. The Greek word for "church" is ἐκκλησία (*ekklesia*). Note that *ekklesis* is from the verb *ekkaleo*, which means to call out.

The Greek word ἐκλεκτός (*eklektos*) is from the verb *eklego*, which means to pick out. There is a difference between calling, which may be resisted, and election (Matt 22:14). Those who respond to the gospel call become the elect, which is the church. William Klein surveyed 1 Peter and concluded,

> We find no hint of the selection of some individuals to be saved. The only individual elected is Christ, the One appointed to his task as redeemer. Though we do find references to God's will in 1 Peter, they concern God's desire or wish for his people to act. Or, God may will (in a determinative sense) his people to suffer, but they must continue their virtuous conduct knowing that God has not forsaken them. The choice of who realizes salvation is not

linked to God's will in 1 Peter.[194]

Wesley summarized the biblical doctrine of predestination,

1. He that believeth shall be saved from the guilt and power of sin.
2. He that endureth to the end shall be saved eternally.[195]

Foreknowledge is not connected to predestination

John Wesley pointed out that strictly speaking there is no foreknowledge or afterknowledge with God, "but all things are known to Him as present from eternity to eternity."[196] Wesley is merely stating that God sees time in its entirety. It is process theology which removes God from eternity by limiting him to the present. They prefer to describe God as "everlasting," regarding the word "eternal" as Neoplatonism. But Deuteronomy 33:27 uses both words to describe God. He is both transcendent or outside time and immanent, acting within history. Murphree argued that God can be active in time without being confined to time.[197]

God through his foreknowledge knew that we would sin and need a Savior. So in v 20, Christ was chosen before creation. He was the Lamb that was slain from the creation of the world (Rev 13:8). The only other place the noun πρόγνωσις

---

[194]Klein, *The New Chosen People*, 247.

[195]Wesley, *Notes*, 608.

[196]Wesley, *Notes*, 608.

[197]Murphree, *Divine Paradoxes*, 28]. See also Reasoner, *Holy Living*, 2:778.

(*prognosis*) is used is Acts 2:23, and it also refers to the crucifixion of Christ. As a verb προγινώσις occurs in Acts 26:5; Romans 8:29; 11:2; 2 Peter 3:17.

However, Wayne Grudem gave three arguments that *foreknowledge* was actually *predestination*.[198] John MacArthur also insists that "foreknowledge involves God's predetermining to have a relationship with some individuals, based on His eternal plan."[199] But these arguments reflect their Calvinism and not the meaning of the word "foreknowledge."

The normal meaning for the word *prognosis* is simple prior knowledge. Any determinism implied must be demonstrated. Therefore, if Peter meant predestination, why did he use the word *prognosis* when he could have utilized the Greek word προορίζω (*prohorizo*) which does mean to mark out boundaries beforehand?[200]

William Klein explained that the crucifixion of Jesus was according to God's plan and foreknowledge, which he had revealed to his prophets, but Peter is emphasizing prior knowledge more than prior determination. "When we connect God's foreknowledge of Christ with the plan of redemption, we cannot deny the factor of prior determination." But when Peter refers to our election, he is speaking corporately. "We find no hint of the selection of some individuals to be saved. The only individual elected is Christ, the One appointed to his task as redeemer."[201] Thus, Christ is the elect, and all who trust in him become the elect corporately.

---

[198] Grudem, *TNTC*, 85.

[199] MacArthur, *1 Peter*, 20.

[200] προορίζω occurs in Acts 4:28; Rom 8:29-30; 1 Cor 2:7; Eph 1:5, 11.

[201] Klein, *The New Chosen People*, 233-247.

Whedon declared that foreknowledge does not imply divine purpose. It simply means knowledge beforehand. "God's foreknowledge always precedes election; and our apostle here teaches that the election is grounded upon it."[202]

Salvation begins with God's preliminary grace. But a human response must follow God's initiative. Jesus explained that while many are called, few are chosen (Matt 22:14). Wesley explained, "First, God works; therefore you *can* work. Secondly, God works; therefore you *must* work."[203] Joseph Benson wrote that we make God's calling effectual by obeying it.[204]

However, John Calvin taught that the call of God was irresistible, and the election of God was unconditional. Calvin commented on this verse,

> God effectually calls whom he has preordained to life in his secret counsel before the foundation of the world; and he also carries on the perpetual course of calling through grace alone. But as he has chosen us, and calls us for this end, that we may be pure and spotless in his presence; purity of life is not improperly called the evidence and proof of election, by which the faithful may not only testify to others that they are the children of God, but also confirm themselves in this confidence.

In a previous paragraph, Calvin addressed the perennial

---

[202]Whedon, *Commentary*, 5:193.

[203]Wesley, "On Working Out Your Own Salvation," Sermon #85, 3.2.

[204]Benson, *Notes*, 5:634.

struggle within Calvinism regarding assurance of election. He explained, "One proof that we have been really elected, and not in vain called by the Lord, if a good conscience and integrity of life correspond with our profession of faith."

In order to understand Calvin, it is necessary to understand that he taught both a general call and an effectual call. Only the elect are effectually called. Here he explained that a good conscience and a life of integrity were evidence of an effectual calling and thus of unconditional election.

But then he denies that "the stability of our calling and election depends on good works," since God's election is based on grace.[205]

Joseph Hill, the Puritan commentator writing in Matthew Henry's commentary, said that it is the duty of believers to make their election sure. But if election is unconditional, the believer can only attempt to assure himself that he is, in fact, truly elect. Hill explained,

> It requires a great deal of diligence and labor to make sure our calling and election; there must be a very close examination of ourselves, a very narrow search and strict enquiry, whether we are thoroughly converted, our mind enlightened, our wills renewed, and our whole souls changed as to the bent and inclination thereof; and to come to a fixed certainty in this requires the utmost diligence, and cannot be attained and kept without divine assistance.

Hill explained why this assurance of election is so difficult.

---

[205] Calvin, *Commentary*, 22:376-377.

None can look into the book of God's eternal counsels and decrees; but, inasmuch as *whom God did predestinate those he also called*, if we can find we are effectually called, we may conclude we are chosen to salvation.[206]

But Calvin taught that the nonelect may demonstrate "temporary faith." William Perkins even developed five degrees of ineffectual calling of the reprobate. In his evaluation of this teaching, R. T. Kendall concluded that the doctrines of limited atonement and temporary faith do not provide much assurance.[207]

Essentially, one has been effectually called *if* he perseveres. But it is hard to persevere if one has no certain knowledge that he is truly called. As a modern Calvinist, R. C. Sproul articulates the assurance that has attracted many to Calvinism. Yet, his confident assertion that nothing can frustrate God's sovereign election flounders with the theological underpinnings that it is very difficult to ascertain whether one is truly elect. And it contradicts the command given by Peter that we have a responsibility to confirm God choosing us in the provision of salvation. Sproul wrote,

> We can do nothing to make an eternal decree of God sure. When God chooses to save someone, his or her election is absolutely certain. God does not choose to save people and then let them decide. There would be no election if that were the case. People

---

[206]Hill, *Matthew Henry's Commentary*, 6:1040.

[207]Kendall, *Calvin and English Calvinism*, chapter five, "William Perkins's Doctrine of Temporary Faith," 67-76. See also Reasoner, *Romans*, 2:52-55.

would thereby be electing themselves with God standing by as an impotent spectator. If God chooses to elect someone, that election must come to pass. Nothing in heaven or on earth can frustrate the sovereign will of God.[208]

Thus, Calvinism advocates three doctrines which are in tension, if not contradictory:

- unconditional election which is *not* based upon works
- the distinction between a general or external call and an effectual call which *is* evidenced by "purity of life"
- and that sin always remains in the regenerate

Therefore, they conclude that the evidence of election is actually the *desire* to be pure and holy. Romans 7:14-25 describes all Christians and no Christian can rise above the "miserable-sinner Christianity."[209]

While Arminian doctrine teaches that God is sovereign, he can elect not to exercise that sovereignty. While it is not his will that anyone should perish, he allows sinners to perish against his will. While God initiates the salvation process, Peter teaches that we must confirm both God's calling and his election.

The NET Bible footnote declares that in soteriological contexts when God is the subject, the verb *calling* always carries the nuance of effectual calling. The footnote continues, "Calling takes place at the moment of conversion, while

---

[208]Sproul, *1-2 Peter*, 220.

[209]Reasoner, *Holy Living*, 1:390-411.

election takes place in eternity past."[210] But this is nothing more than Calvinistic dogma. Election is corporate. Many are called, but only those who respond to the gospel call are incorporated into the elect.

While systematic theology attempts to define a chronological order, in which election comes first and then calling, Peter apparently uses both words here as synonyms. He does not explain election in a pre-temporal or predetermined sense. "Election implies that these Christians enjoy the status of God's chosen ones. However, only a life of faithfulness demonstrates the validity of its application to individuals."[211]

Although Calvinism advocates the doctrine of unconditional election, Peter states a condition. "For if you do these things, you will never fall" (2 Pet 1:10). The present tense participle suggests a conditional and continual doing. Coke explained that God did not decree that anyone should stumble and fall.

> Faith was the condition on which they were called into the Christian church, and elected to be of the number of God's people here upon earth. And they were so called and elected, with a view to their obtaining eternal salvation: for, as Christians, they had all things pertaining to a godly life, and the best advantages for preparing for everlasting life: but the bestowing of that life, even upon such as are called and elected, is suspended upon the condition that they, according to the measure of grace given them, and the opportunities afforded them, do internally

---

[210]NET Bible, 2368.

[211]Klein, *The New Chosen People*, 253.

and externally exercise their graces and virtues. Otherwise, both their calling and election will prove in vain, and they will finally miss of a happy immortality.[212]

Peter also uses the most decisive negative possible in the Greek language, which can be translated "never at any time." But the promise of "never at any time" is conditioned by the exhortation to make every effort or to take pains *(spoudazo)* to confirm, ratify, or guarantee their faith.[213] "Believers make their election sure by obeying Christ and deliberately growing in grace."[214]

The implication is that if we do not follow through on our commitment, we *will* fall. Daniel A. Whedon added, "In which case the election would become null, and their rejection of God would be followed by his rejection of them from his elect people."[215]

But Calvinism holds that if God is sovereign, whatever he decrees is predestined to happen. Therefore, they infer that God has two wills, his desires and his decrees.[216] But the Greek words θέλμα (*thelma*) and βουλή (*boule*) do not bear out any distinction between his revealed will and his "dark side."

While Jesus taught us to pray for God's will (*thelma*) to be done on earth, we cannot conclude that whatever happens

---

[212]Coke, *Commentary*, 6:828.

[213]Green, *BECNT*, 201.

[214]Powers, *NBBC*, 187.

[215]Whedon, *Commentary*, 5:230.

[216]Schreiner, *1,2 Peter, Jude*, 381-382.

on earth is necessarily his will. Although God's sovereignty is an accepted truth, it does not necessarily follow that his will is always determinative, compulsory, or coerced. He made mankind in his image and likeness, and part of that image and likeness is true libertarian freedom of choice, which is demonstrated in Luke 7:30, where the Pharisees reject God's purpose (*boule*).

Calvinists, however, reason that if all are not saved, it is only because God has not decreed all mankind to be saved. But God's hidden will cannot contradict his secret decree. All that we know about God is what he has revealed, and nothing in Scripture implies two contrary wills.

Coke wrote that God is sincere. "He has no secret will contrary to, and inconsistent with his revealed will. . . . Hence it appears evidently, that God has not absolutely decreed the damnation of any man; but men, by their own folly and wickedness, bring upon themselves misery and destruction."[217] However, Calvin argued,

> But it could be asked here, if God does not want any to perish, why is it that so many do perish? To this my answer is, that no mention is here made of the hidden purpose of God, according to which the reprobate are doomed to their own ruin, but only of his will as made known to us in the gospel. For God there stretches forth his hand without a difference to all, but lays hold only of those, to lead them to himself, whom he has chosen before the foundation of the world.[218]

---

[217]Coke, *Commentary*, 6:844.

[218]Calvin, *Commentary*, 22:419-420.

If God has a hidden purpose, why was it not also hidden from Calvin? When the logical inconsistencies of Calvinism threaten to destroy their whole system, we are told God's election and human believing cannot be put into a logical relationship to one another.[219] Thus, when their golden chain of logic snaps, they dismiss and adopt a position of agnosticism. In his book *Evangelism and the Sovereignty of God*, J. I. Packer advocated the necessity of evangelism. He affirmed both the doctrines of divine sovereignty and human responsibility, which he labeled an *antinomy*. He explained, "An antinomy exists when a pair of principles stand side by side, seemingly irreconcilable, yet both undeniable."[220] Calvinists rightly declare that Scripture does not contradict itself. But when they make irreconcilable statements about what the Bible teaches, they simply declare that it is an *antinomy*. The use of this word explains nothing. While Wesleyan-Arminians affirm that the Bible teaches both divine sovereignty and human responsibility, the real purpose of Packer's book is to reconcile the biblical mandate to evangelize with Calvinistic determinism.

However, Packer cited a dialogue between Charles Simeon and John Wesley.[221] This exchange alone is sufficient to establish that Wesley taught salvation by grace alone and not by human works.

Packer affirmed his belief in a limited atonement, yet wants to avoid any discussion of the implications for evange-

---

[219]Carson, *Divine Sovereignty and Human Responsibility*, 201-222.

[220]Packer, *Evangelism and the Sovereignty of God*, 18.

[221]Packer, *Evangelism and the Sovereignty of God*, 13-14.

lism.[222] Although Packer affirmed his belief in absolute predestination, he responded that this doctrine does not have any bearing on the necessity or urgency of evangelism. Even if God has secretly purposed to damn the non-elect, since none can be saved without the Gospel, "whatever we may believe about election, the fact remains that evangelism is necessary."[223]

> Whatever we may believe about election, and, for that matter, about the extent of the atonement, the fact remains that God in the gospel really does offer Christ and promise justification to "whosoever will." … We should not be held back by the thought that if they are not elect, they will not believe us, and our efforts to convert them will fail. This is true; but it is none of our business, and should make no difference to our action.[224]

Packer proceeded to affirm the notion of effectual calling as the outworking of God's purpose of election. He affirmed that this grace is irresistible, but also claimed that it is the sinner's own fault that he is not saved.[225] Elsewhere Packer declared that only those who receive the gift of faith will come to Christ and abide in him.[226] Packer does not explain why it is a sinner's fault that he has not received the gift of

---

[222]Packer, *Evangelism and the Sovereignty of God*, 67-69.

[223]Packer, *Evangelism and the Sovereignty of God*, 94-97.

[224]Packer, *Evangelism and the Sovereignty of God*, 100; 99.

[225]Packer, *Evangelism and the Sovereignty of God*, 113-114; 105.

[226]Packer, "Faith," *Baker's Dictionary of Theology*, 210.

faith. Packer admitted,

> It is true that God has from all eternity chosen whom He will save. It is true that Christ came specifically to save those whom the Father had given Him. But it is also true That Christ offers Himself freely to all men as their Savior, and guarantees to bring to glory everyone who trust in Him as such. Some fear that a doctrine of eternal election and reprobation involves the possibility that Christ will not receive some of those who desire to receive Him, because they are not elect. The "comfortable words" of the gospel promises, however, absolutely exclude this possibility. As our Lord elsewhere affirmed, in emphatic and categorical terms: "Him that cometh to me I will *in no wise* cast out."[227]

His advice to Calvinists is, basically, to preach like Arminians. But how can the Gospel sincerely be preached to whosoever will, when the preacher has accepted Calvinistic presuppositions? Lloyd-Jones declared, "The *whosoever* is determined by God."[228] However, if God did not determine to offer salvation to all, then everyone cannot be saved. The fact is that God determined *whosoever* may be saved.

Calvinists interpret 2 Peter 3:9 to mean that God is not willing that any class of people should perish. Since Peter was writing to the Jews, God was not willing that any of them should perish. All who are within this class of people will be saved. Yet it is usually Wesleyan Arminians who hold to

---

[227]Packer, *Evangelism and the Sovereignty of God*, 102.

[228]Lloyd-Jones, *Saving Faith*, 378.

corporate election! It seems that the only way Calvinists can avoid the clear implications of Peter's word from the Lord is to borrow the Wesleyan doctrine of corporate election as the key to this particular passage. Inconsistently, however, they reject this doctrine in any other context.

R. C. Sproul wrote that the real question concerns the word *any*.

> The assumption that people read into the text is that "any" refers to everyone or any person. If that is the case, then Peter would be saying that God sovereignly is not willing that anyone should perish. Sometimes when an objection is raised to a position, the argument brought forth proves more than the objectors want it to prove. The Arminian objection to the Reformed view of this text is that if God is not willing that anyone should perish, then it proves universalism. It would prove that everyone is saved and that no one perishes, but how can that be squared with everything else the Bible teaches to the contrary?

Thus, Sproul dodges the implication of his Calvinism through his distortion of Arminianism. But Arminians are not universalists. Universalism is a heretical teaching that everyone will be saved. The conclusion of universalism is that there is no hell. This conclusion is related to the doctrine of conditional immortality, which holds that the unsaved cease to exist after they die, and annihilationism, which holds that hell consumes the sinner.

In contrast, biblical Arminians hold to a universal atonement, meaning that the substitutionary death of Christ was sufficient to save the entire human race. But the work of

Christ must be appropriated through faith. Thus, only those who believe are saved.

Sproul, however, proceeded to define *any* and *us* in the passage as a reference to the elect. He concluded,

> No passage in all Scripture more strongly defends unconditional election than this one. God sovereignly decrees that none of His elect will perish and that all whom He has chosen will come to Him. They will repent. They will come in faith to Him, because election is not in the abstract. Election is unto faith, repentance, and salvation.[229]

Yet the same verse goes on to reveal that God wants *all* to repent — the antithesis of *perish*. The word *all* (πᾶς - *pas*) means *everyone*. Daniel Powers explained, "There is no grammatical or contextual indication that everyone is limited to a select group of people (i.e. those of you). Rather, *everyone* indicates God has made *repentance* and salvation possible for every person."[230] Actually, it was the Gnostics who first taught a limited salvation, available only to the "spiritual," whom they identified as themselves.

In the face of 2 Peter 1:5-10, which warns believers that we make our calling and election sure through our obedience, Calvinism teaches the exact opposite. They affirm that election is unconditional. In the face of Peter's clear statement in 2 Peter 3:9 that God is *not* willing that any should perish, Calvinism teaches that God's secret will is the exact opposite. They affirm that only the elect can be saved — that the elect

---

[229]Sproul, *1-2 Peter*, 278-279.

[230]Powers, *NBBC*, 233.

are predestined to believe, repent, and be saved. This is another gospel. And it provides no "good news" at all for the non-elect.

Wesley argued that if the saved are only those who are elected by grace, God has, in effect, decreed not to save the rest. Whether it is called election, preterition, predestination, or reprobation, it all amounts to the same thing.

> By virtue of an eternal, unchangeable, irresistible decree of God, one part of mankind are infallibly saved, and the rest infallibly damned; it being impossible that any of the former should be damned, or that any of the latter should be saved.[231]

Apparently God was willing for Gentiles to be lost, since many are lost. This perversion of the gospel is wrong at every point.

---

[231] Wesley, "Free Grace," Sermon #110, §9.

A THEOLOGY OF ELECTION

Having studied the Scripture first, we are now in a better position to draw some conclusions. Within systematic theology there are five major views on election.

1. Calvinism affirms unconditional personal election. Writing on Ephesians 1:8-9 Calvin stated, "God was moved by no external cause; He Himself and in Himself was author and cause of our being elected while yet we were not created."[232]

God's purpose to saving the world is made known to everyone by a proclamation of the free offer of grace. The call must be as universal as the benefit of a universal atonement. Thus, the Spirit's calling is efficacious since he makes all who hear it conscious of their responsibility and capable of obedience. However, it is not irresistible. Those who accept the divine call are the elect. "Election always presupposes the call; but the call does not always issue in election."[233] Jesus explained, "For many are invited, but few are chosen" (Matt 22:14). He warned that the Jews "refuse to come to me to have life" (John 5:40). Like their fathers, they "always resist the Holy Spirit" (Acts 7:51). Judas was one of the elect, yet he

---

[232]Calvin, *Eternal Predestination*, 69.

[233]Pope, *Compendium*, 2:345.

forfeited his election (John 6:70). Therefore, we must make our calling and election sure (2 Pet 1:10) by enduring to the end (Matt 24:13).

Calvinism, however, teaches that a general or external call is to be preached universally, but that the call is effectual or inward only in the elect. Robert Haldane concluded that the call in Romans 2:4 was merely an external call "without any saving effect."

> From this it evidently follows that God externally calls many to whom He has not purposed to give the grace of conversion. It also follows that it cannot be said that when God thus externally calls persons on whom it is not His purpose to bestow grace, His object is only to render them inexcusable. For if that were the case, the Apostle would not have spoken of the riches of His goodness and forbearance, and long-suffering, - terms which would not be applicable, if, by such a call, it was intended merely to render men inexcusable.[234]

This seems to create a moral dilemma for the conscious Calvinistic evangelist which borders on false advertizing. Louis Berkhof, a Calvinistic theologian, wrote that missionaries cannot

> go out and give their hearers the assurance that Christ died for each one of them and that God intends to save each one; but it does mean that they can bring the joyful tidings that Christ died for sinners, that He invites them to come unto Him, and

---

[234] Haldane, *Exposition*, 78-79.

that He offers salvation to all those who truly repent of their sins and accept him with a living faith.[235]

In other words the evangelist can issue a general call, but it will be irresistible only for those who are elect. This destroys the "good news" of the gospel for the reprobate or non-elect.

Actually this call is not irresistible. Jesus taught that "many are called, but few are chosen" (Matt 22:14). "Therefore, my brothers, be all the more eager to make your calling and election sure. For if you do these things you will never fall" (2 Pet 1:10). Oden explained, "The freedom to hear implies also the freedom not to hear, or to hear and to decline the invitation."[236]

No one can come to Christ unless the Father draws him (John 6:44). When Christ is preached as the object of our faith, the Holy Spirit drawn all men to Christ (John 12:32). While this is a supernatural tug, the Greek verb ἑλκύω (*helkuo*) does not mean that God irresistibly draws the elect. There is no implication that the drawing is either select or irresistible.

In Luke 14:23 the church is commissioned to persuade sinners to come to God's house. However, the verb ἀναγκάζω (*anagkazo*) cannot imply forcing them against their will.

Romans 2:4-5 teaches that the purpose of God's kindness, tolerance, and patience is to lead the sinner toward repentance. While the context here refers specifically to the Jew, it is obvious that they are not unconditionally elect. It should also be noted that ἄγω, which is translated "lead" does

---

[235]Berkhof, *Systematic Theology*, 463.

[236]Oden, *The Transforming Grace of God*, 49.

not necessarily imply the idea of force or that grace is irresistible. Charles Hodge objected to the statement,"God leads, but man *may* refuse to be led."[237] Thomas Summers protested, "Leading implies voluntary following; but Hodge says, God makes willing! Were these wretches made willing? Why will men allow themselves to be so biased by peculiar dogmas."[238]

The word *also* in Romans 2:14-15 indicts the Gentiles as well. The preliminary grace of God informs their conscience to the extent that they are also without excuse if they resist.

Scripture does not distinguish between a general call and an effectual call. Thomas Coke said "effectual calling" was a distinction which theologians have invented, without any warrant from Scripture.[239]

While Calvinism teaches that the call of God is irresistible and the election of God is unconditional, Peter teaches we must confirm both. Then he states a condition. For doing these things, you will by no means ever fall. The implication is that if we do not follow through on our commitment that we will fall.

But what does it mean to fall? 2 Peter 1:11 explains that those who do not fall away will be welcomed into heaven. The implication is that those who do fall away will not be welcomed into heaven.

Calvinists object that God is sovereign and his call cannot be resisted. We affirm the sovereignty of God, but believe that God can choose to limit his power. The call is an invitation, not a conscription.

Karl Barth pointed out that the first edition of Calvin's

---

[237]Hodge, *Romans*, 48-49.

[238]Summers, *Romans*, 17-18.

[239]Coke, *Commentary*, 5:92.

Institutes referred election primarily to the church. But by the final edition Calvin taught the particular election and reprobation which was unconditional.[240]

Barth warned that we should be wary of jumping to the conclusion that this election to be holy and blameless is necessarily a double election with a corresponding election to condemnation.

> Can there be, may there be, must there be *individuals* chosen for condemnation in addition to those chosen for blessedness? That is the question behind these interpretations. Yes, says Calvin. . . . claiming that this teaching has "such great profit from it that it had been much better if we had never been born than be ignorant of what St. Paul shows here" and even further that, "it were better that the whole world should go to confusion than that this doctrine should be reduced to silence."

Barth argued that the focus of Ephesians 1:4 was God, not man. As a Calvinist, Barth concluded that, "We must first understand Paul, bypassing Calvin, in order to understand Paul by way of Calvin."[241] God does not arbitrarily decree that certain individuals will be saved and all others be damned. Whedon argued that God's election was based upon his foreknowledge.[242] The emphasis is not on the selection from out of the mass of humanity, but on the end for which the choice

---

[240] Barth, *Church Dogmatics* II/2: 307.

[241] Barth, *Ephesians*, 94-96. In the block quote I have supplied the English translation. Barth quoted Calvin in French.

[242] Whedon, *Commentary*, 4:257.

was made.²⁴³ Wiley wrote that the doctrine of election cannot be separated from the doctrine and experience of holiness.

> It is not, therefore, in the so-called "hidden counsels" of God that we are to look for the evidences of our election, but in the visible life of holiness and righteousness.²⁴⁴

Benson wrote,

> He that believes is not only elected to eternal salvation if he endure to the end, but is fore-appointed of God to walk in holiness and righteousness, to the praise of his glory.²⁴⁵

God declares in Acts 9:15 that Paul was his chosen instrument. The word used is ἐκλογή (*ekloge* - from the verb *eklegomai*). But while Paul knew he was elect, he stated in 1 Corinthians 9:27 that it was possible for him to become ἀδόκιμος (*adolimos* - reprobate).

2. While Barth's criticism of Calvin is valid, Barth went too far the opposite direction — apparently taught a universal and unconditional election in Christ. Thus, God has elected the entire human race for salvation in Jesus Christ. When this is coupled with the Calvinistic doctrine of irresistible grace,

---

²⁴³Abbott, *ICC*, 6.

²⁴⁴Wiley, *Ephesians*, 40-41.

²⁴⁵Benson, *Notes*, 5:303.

it leads to the heresy of universalism.[246]

His son, Markus Barth wrote that the church includes virtually all who are still unbelievers. Jesus Christ is not only head of the church, he is as much head also of every man, "whether that man believes in Christ or not."[247] Yet *all things* in v 10 does not mean universal salvation. "The dividing wall which Jesus has abolished is not the barrier which separates the world *from* the church; it is the barrier which segregates groups and individuals from one another *within* the church."[248]

Thomas F. Torrance, a leading Reformed theologian of the twentieth century and student of Barth, held that election begins in eternity in the person of Jesus Christ, who is both the subject and object of election. Christ is the Elect One, meaning that God chose him to reconcile estranged humanity. The eternal election of God first entered into time by first electing Israel and then narrowing that election down to a single Israelite, Jesus of Nazareth.

> *Prothesis* [purpose] means that not only in Christ the beloved are we eternally loved and elected, but that Christ is the way in which we are loved and elected.

---

[246] Barth, *Church Dogmatics* II/2, 3-93. He denies this conclusion in pp. 417-418, but it is logically implied. Galli evaluates the evidence in his biography [*Karl Barth*, 119-121]. See also Talbott, "Universal Reconciliation," 206-261 and Olson, "Election is for Everyone," 40-43.

[247] Barth, *Broken Wall*, 110. In *Israel and the Church*, Markus Barth claims that since faith is not mentioned in Eph 2:14-15 that this new entity is not limited to Jewish and Gentile-born Christians only [p. 95].

[248] Stott, *God's New Society*, 43.

He is the way, the door, and there is no other way to the Father, no other door to salvation, than he.[249]

For Torrance, the gospel is that in Christ all people have been unconditionally elected to communion with God. Torrance called the notion of a limited atonement "heresy." He also rejected the Arminian view that the atonement *potentially* saves all. Instead, the atonement is objectively sufficient and efficacious for everyone.[250]

3. The classic Arminian position is the conditional election of individuals. This position is advocated by Free Will Baptist scholars such as Robert E. Picirilli and F. Leroy Forlines.[251] I stand with them, but I believe there is also a corporate aspect to election.

4. Corporate election for service. Clark Pinnock represents a fourth view, that election is corporate and that God has chosen the church to proclaim the Gospel to the world. He declared that election is not for privilege but for service.[252] William Klein takes this position.[253] This is also the position of Jack Cottrell within the Stone-Campbell Restoration Movement.[254] Cottrell believes that it was not Paul's purpose

---

[249]Torrance, *Incarnation*, 179.

[250]Torrance, *Atonement*, 187.

[251]Picirilli, *Grace, Faith, Free Will*, 50-53; Forlines, *Classical Arminianism*, 122-128.

[252]Pinnock, "Divine Election," 276-314.

[253]Klein, *New Chosen People*, 33; 44.

[254]Cottrell, "Conditional Election," 51-73.

in Romans 9 to explain election to salvation at all.[255]

William MacDonald called Ephesians 1:3-14 the most definite passage on election in the New Testament and wrote that Divine election is God's decision to sum up all things in Christ. Thus, Christ is God's Chosen One and we are incorporated into Christ.[256]

Muddiman explained that the election of the pre-existent Son before the creation of the world is itself the election of those who are to become incorporate in him. Thus, the elect are those who believe in the One who is the unique object of God's elective love.[257] However, the object of God's choice in v 4 is not Christ, but us.

I have no real problem with this interpretation, but it contributes virtually nothing to our understanding of whether salvation is conditional or unconditional.

5. While all Arminians affirm conditional election regarding salvation, the Wesleyan-Arminian position also tends to emphasize the corporate nature of election. Joseph Benson wrote,

> For the election spoken of in the New Testament is not the election of individuals, out of the mass of mankind, to repent, believe, and obey, passing by the rest; but it is the election of such as are already possessed of faith, love, and a new nature, to be the people and children of God.

---

[255]Cottrell, *Romans*, 2:42.

[256]MacDonald, "Biblical Doctrine of Election," 219-226. See also Lincoln, *WBC*, 42:23, 33-34, 44.

[257]Muddiman, *Ephesians*, 67.

Benson went on to say that the elect made their calling and election sure by aspiring after a larger measure of faith and love, and by enduring to the end.[258]

Richard Watson observed that the Synod of Dort quoted Ephesians 1:4-6 as the leading proof of personal election. However, Watson contended that this passage did not refer to the personal election of individual believers, but to the collective election of the whole body of Christians.[259]

H. Orton Wiley declared that he held to *class* predestination — "the elect are those that are in Christ."[260] Thus, the *elect* are a class of people and that class is not restricted only to Jews. It is composed of all who have accepted Jesus Christ as Lord, whether Jew or Gentile.

Vanderhoof said the emphasis is not so much on choosing as on the condition of the choosing. "God made the choice that those who were to be his would be his through Christ."[261]

McClintock and Strong wrote that a just exegesis of Romans 9-11

> shows that they can be interpreted only of collective election, not of personal election. The apostle does, indeed, treat of unconditional election in this discourse, but it is of unconditional collective election.[262]

---

[258]Benson, *Notes*, 5:301-302.

[259]Watson, *Theological Institutes*, 2:349.

[260]Henry, "Debate Over Divine Election," 3.

[261]Vanderhoof, *Asbury Bible Commentary*, 1052.

[262]McClintock and Strong, *Cyclopedia*, 3:129. In this article they also cite Watson, *Institutes*, 2:312-325.

John Fletcher argued that the predestination and election described in Ephesians 1 refers

> only of God's predestinating and electing THE GENTILES IN GENERAL (and among them the Ephesians) to share the prerogatives of the Christian dispensation.[263]

Corporate election is also upheld by non-Methodists such as Roger Forster and Paul Marston who wrote that Romans 9-11 "is talking about nations and not about individuals."[264] Cranfield agrees.[265] Robert Shank also holds this view, arguing primarily from Ephesians.

> Obviously, the corporate body of the elect is comprised of individuals. But the election is primarily corporate and only secondarily particular. The thesis that election is corporate, as Paul understood it and viewed in the Ephesian doxology, is supported by the whole context of his epistle.[266]

Thus, the doctrine of election has four components:

- God chose Christ to be the savior of the world
- Our election hinges on our acceptance of Christ and our trust in him
- God chooses all who are trusting in Christ

---

[263]Fletcher, *Works*, 2:119-126.

[264]Forester and Marston, *God's Strategy in Human History*, 59.

[265]Cranfield, *ICC*, 2:450.

[266]Shank, *Elect in the Son*, 45-55.

- The church is the corporate body of those who are in Christ.

Thus, Jesus Christ is God's Elect. Those who are trusting in Jesus Christ are personally saved from sin. Because God knows in advance who will trust in Christ and persevere, they are designated as his *elect*. The church of Jesus Christ is comprised of all those who are saved through Christ and thus, the church is the corporate body of the elect.

This conclusion squares with the general tenor of Scripture, as well as the consensus of the early church. Jacob Arminius did not concoct this theological construct. Instead, he articulated the general consensus of the church before Augustine and Calvin. John Wesley championed this consensus teaching in the eighteenth century.

While the followers of Arminius, the Remonstrants, eventually became too liberal and while the Methodist Church ultimately departed from Scripture and Wesley, this classic Wesleyan-Arminian theology, based on serious scriptural exegesis, has fewer exegetical problems that does Calvinism.

BIBLIOGRAPHY

Abbott, T. K. *The Epistle to the Ephesians and to the Colossians: The International Critical Commentary on the Holy Scriptures of the Old and New Testaments.* Edinburgh: T&T Clark, 1897.

Ambrosiaster. *Ancient Christian Tests: Commentaries on Galatians-Philemon.* Gerald L. Bray, ed. Downers Grove, IL: InterVarsity, 2009.

Arminius, James. *The Works of James Arminius: The London Edition.* 3 vols. Transl by James and William Nichols. 1828. Reprint, Grand Rapids: Baker 1996.

Augustine, "A Treatise On Rebuke and Grace." *Nicene and Post Nicene Fathers.* First Series. Vol. 5. 1887. Philip Schaff, ed. Reprint, Grand Rapids: Eerdmans, 1978.

Augustine. *City of God.* Transl by J. F. Shaw. *The Nicene and Post-Nicene Fathers.* First Series. Vol. 2. Philip Schaff, ed. 1886-1879. Reprint, Grand Rapids: Eerdmans, 1978-1979.

Barnhouse, Donald Grey. *Expositions of Bible Doctrines Taking the Epistle to the Romans as a Point of Departure.* 10 vols. Grand Rapids: Eerdmans, 1952-1964.

Barth, Karl. *Church Dogmatics* II/2. Transl by G. W. Bromiley. Edinburgh: T&T Clark, 1957.

_____. *The Epistle to the Ephesians.* R. David Nelson, ed. Ross M. Wright, transl. Grand Rapids: Baker 2017.

Barth, Markus. *The Broken Wall: A Study of the Epistle to the Ephesians.* Chicago: Judson, 1959.

_____. *Israel and the Church: Contribution to a Dialogue Vital for Peace.* Richmond: John Knox Press, 1969.

Beet, J. Agar. *A Commentary on St. Paul's Epistle to the Romans.* 10th ed. 1902. Reprint, Salem, OH: Allegheny, 1982.

Benson, Joseph. *The Holy Bible, with Notes, All the Marginal Readings, Summaries, and the Date of Every Transaction.* 2nd ed. 5 vols. 1811-1818. Reprint, New York: Carlton & Phillips, 1856.

_____. *Sermons and Plans of Sermons on Many of the Most Important Texts of Holy Scripture.* 7 vols. Baltimore: Armstrong & Plaskitt, 1824-1828.

Berkhof, Louis. *Systematic Theology.* Grand Rapids: Eerdmans, 1941.

Binney, Amos and Daniel Steele. *The People's Commentary.* New York: Nelson & Phillips, 1879.

Boice, James. *Romans.* 4 vols. Grand Rapids: Baker, 1991-1995.

Blum, Edwin A. "1-2 Peter." *The Expositor's Bible Commentary.* Vol. 12. Frank E. Gaebelein, ed. Grand Rapids: Zondervan, 1981.

Boetnner, Loraine. *The Reformed Doctrine of Predestination.* Philadelphia: Presbyterian & Reformed, 1965.

Bray, Gerald, ed. *Ancient Christian Commentary on Scripture: Romans.* Vol. 6. Thomas C. Oden, ed. Downers Grove, IL: InterVarsity, 1998.

Bridges, Jerry. "Don't Look Back." *Tabletalk* 26:1 (January 2002) 14-16.

Bruce, F. F. *Tyndale New Testament Commentaries: Romans.* Vol. 6. Grand Rapids: Eerdmans, 1963.

Burwash, Nathanael. *A Handbook of the Epistle of St. Paul to the Romans.* 2nd ed. Toronto: William Briggs, 1900.

Calvin, John. *Calvin's Commentaries.* 22 vols. 1540-1565. Reprint, Grand Rapids: Baker, 1979.

_____. *Institutes of Christian Religion.* 2 vols. 1559. Henry Beveridge trans. Reprint, Grand Rapids: Eerdmans, 1995.

_____. *Concerning the Eternal Predestination of God.* J. K. S. Reid, translator. 1552. Reprint, Louisville: John Knox, 1997.

Carson, D. A. *Divine Sovereignty and Human Responsibility.* Grand Rapids: Baker, 1994.

Clarke, Adam. *The Holy Bible: Containing the Old and New Testaments: The Text Carefully Printed from the Most Correct Copies of the Present Authorized Translations, Including the Marginal reading and Parallel Texts; with a Commentary and Critical Notes, Designed as a help to a better Understanding of the Sacred Writings.* 6 vols. 1811-1825. Reprint, Nashville, Abingdon, 1950.

Coke, Thomas. *A Commentary on the Whole Bible.* 6 vols. London: G. Whitefield, 1801-1803.

Cottrell, Jack. *The College Press NIV Commentary: Romans.* 2 vols. College Press: Joplin, MO: 1998.

_____. "Conditional Election." *Grace Unlimited.* Clark H. Pinnock, ed. Minneapolis: Bethany House, 1975.

Cranfield, C. E. B. *International Critical Commentary: A Critical and Exegetical Commentary on the Epistle to the Romans.* 2 vols. Edinburgh: T&T Clark, 1975; 1979.

Cremer, Hermann. *Biblico-Theological Lexicon of New Testament Greek.* Edinburgh: T&T Clark, 1878.

Danne, James. *The Freedom of God.* Grand Rapids: Eerdmans, 1973.

Denney, James. *The Expositor's Greek Testament.* W. Robertson Nicoll, ed. Vol. 2. 1900. Reprint, Grand Rapids: Eerdmans, 1951.

Dunn, James D. G. *Word Biblical Commentary: Romans 1-8.* Vol. 38A. Dallas: Word, 1988.

Duty, Guy. *If Ye Continue*. Minneapolis: Bethany Fellowship, 1966.

Edwards, Mark J. *Ancient Christian Commentary on Scripture: Galatians, Ephesians, Philippians*. Vol. 8. Thomas C. Oden, ed. Downers Grove, IL: InterVarsity, 1999.

Edwards, Jonathan. *Freedom of the Will*. Paul Ramsey, ed. *The Works of Jonathan Edwards*. Vol. 1. New Haven, CT: Yale University Press, 1957.

Fisk, Samuel. *Election and Predestination*. Bicester, UK: Penfold Book & Bible House, 1997.

Fitzmyer, Joseph A. *The Anchor Bible: Romans*. William F. Albright and David Freedman, eds. New York: Doubleday, 1993.

Fletcher, John. *The Works of the Reverend John Fletcher*. 4 vols. 1833. Reprint, Salem, OH: Schmul, 1974.

Forester, Roger T. and Paul V. Marston. *God's Strategy in Human History*. Wheaton, IL: Tyndale, 1973.

Forlines, F. Leroy. *Classical Arminianism*. Nashville: Randall House, 2011.

Frame, John. *Salvation Belongs to the Lord*. Phillipsburg, NJ: P&R Publishing, 2006.

_____. *The Doctrine of God*. Phillipsburg, NJ: Presbyterian & Reformed, 2002.

Galli, Mark. *Karl Barth: An Introductory Biography for Evangelicals*. Grand Rapids: Eerdmans, 2017.

Greathouse, William M. *Beacon Bible Commentary: Romans*. Vol. 8. Kansas City: Beacon Hill, 1968.

Green, Gene L. *Baker Evangelical Commentary on the New Testament: Jude & 2 Peter*. Grand Rapids: Baker, 2008.

Grider, J. Kenneth. *A Wesleyan-Holiness Theology*. Kansas City: Beacon Hill, 1994.

_____. "Predestination as Temporal Only." *Wesleyan Theological Journal* 22:2 (Fall 1987) 56-64.

Grudem, Wayne A. *Tyndale New Testament Commentaries: 1 Peter*. Vol. 17. Grand Rapids: Eerdmans, 1988.

Haldane, Robert. *Exposition of the Epistle to the Romans*. 1847. Reprint, London: Banner of Truth, 1958.

Henry, Carl F. H. "Feature Interview: The Debate Over Divine Election." *Christianity Today* 4:1 (12 October 1959) 3-18.

Hill, Joseph. *Matthew Henry's Commentary on the Whole Bible: 2 Peter*. Vol. 6. 1708-1710. Reprint, McLean, VA: MacDonald, 1985.

Hodge, Charles. *Commentary on the Epistle to the Romans*. 1886. Reprint, Grand Rapids: Eerdmans, 1950.

Hooker, Richard. *Of the Lawes of Ecclesiastical Politie*. 8 vols. 1593-1648.

Kaiser, Walter C. Jr. Peter H. Davids, F. F. Bruce, Manfred T. Brauch. *Hard Sayings of the Bible*. Downers Grove, IL: InterVarsity, 1996.

Käsemann, Ernst. *Commentary on Romans*. G. W. Bromiley, transl. Grand Rapids: Eerdmans, 1980.

Kendall, R. T. *Calvin and English Calvinism to 1649*. London: Oxford University Press, 1979.

Kinlaw, Dennis. "Ephesians 1: Holy Love." http://www.francisasburysociety.com/ephesians-1-holy-love.

Klein, William W. *The New Chosen People*. Grand Rapids: Zondervan, 1990.

Krey, Philip D. W. and Peter D. W. Krey. *Reformation Commentary on Scripture: Romans 9-16*. Vol. 8. Timothy George, ed. Downers Grove, IL: InterVarsity, 2016.

Lewis, C. S. *The Problem of Pain*. New York: MacMillan, 1962.

Lincoln, Andrew T. *Word Biblical Commentary: Ephesians*. Vol. 42. Dallas: Word, 1990.

Lloyd-Jones, D. Martyn. *The Final Perseverance of the Saints: An Exposition of Romans 8:17-39*. Grand Rapids: Zondervan, 1975.

_____. *God's Sovereign Purpose: An Exposition of Romans 9*. Edinburgh: Banner of Truth, 1991.

_____. *Saving Faith: An Exposition of Romans 10*. Edinburgh: Banner of Truth, 1997.

Longking, Joseph. *Notes on the Epistle of Paul the Apostle to the Galatians and Ephesians*. New York: Carlton & Porter, 1863.

MacArthur, John. *The MacArthur New Testament Commentary: Romans 1-8*. Chicago: Moody, 1991.

_____. *The MacArthur New Testament Commentary: 1 Peter*. Chicago: Moody, 2004.

MacDonald, William. "The Biblical Doctrine of Election." *The Grace of God and the Will of Man*. Clark H. Pinnock, ed. Minneapolis: Bethany House, 1989.

Marshall, I. Howard. *Kept by the Power of God*. 3rd ed. Carlisle Cumbria: Paternoster, 1995.

McClintock, John and James Strong. *Cyclopedia of Biblical, Theological, and Ecclesiastical Literature*. 12 vols. 1867-1887. Reprint, Grand Rapids: Baker, 1981.

Mickelsen, A. Berkeley. "Romans." *Wycliffe Bible Commentary*. Everett F. Harrison, ed. Chicago: Moody, 1962.

Moo, Douglas. *The Wycliffe Bible Commentary: Romans 1-8*. Kenneth Barker, ed. Chicago: Moody, 1991.

Moule, Handley C. G. *The Epistle of Paul the Apostle to the Romans*. 5th ed. 1879. Reprint, New York: Armstrong, 1902.

_____. *Studies in Ephesians*. 1893. Reprint, Grand Rapids: Kregel, 1977.

Muddiman, John. *The Epistle to the Ephesians: Black's New Testament Commentaries*. Morna D. Hooker, ed. Peabody, MA: Hendrickson, 2001.

Murphree, Jon Tal. *Divine Paradoxes*. Camp Hill, PA: Christian Publications, 1998.

Murray, John. *The New International Commentary: The Epistle to the Romans*. 2 vols. Ned B. Stonehouse, ed. Grand Rapids: Eerdmans, 1959.

Ness, Christopher. *The Antidote Against Arminianism*. 1600. Reprint, Edmonton, AB: Still Waters Revival Books, 1988.

The NET Bible. Biblical Studies Press, 1996-2005.

Oden, Thomas C. *The Living God: Systematic Theology*. Vol. 1. San Francisco: Harper & Row, 1987.

_____. *The Transforming Power of Grace*. Nashville: Abingdon, 1993.

_____. *John Wesley's Teachings*. 4 vols. Grand Rapids: Zondervan, 2012-2014.

Olson, Roger E. *Arminian Theology*. Downers Grove, IL: InterVarsity, 2006.

_____. "Election is for Everyone." *Christianity Today* 57:1 (Jan/Feb 2013) 40-43.

Oropeza, B. J. *Apostasy in the New Testament Communities: Jews, Gentiles, and the Opponents of Paul: The Pauline Letters*. Vol. 2. Eugene, OR: Cascade, 2012.

Packer, J. I. *Evangelism and the Sovereignty of God*. Downers Grove, IL: InterVarsity, 1961.

_____. "Faith." *Baker's Dictionary of Theology*. Everett F. Harrison, ed. Grand Rapids: Baker, 1960.

Palmer, Edwin. *The Five Points of Calvinism*. Grand Rapids: Baker, 1972.

Patzia, Arthur G. *New International Biblical Commentary: Ephesians, Colossians, Philemon*. Vol. 10. Peabody, MA: Hendrickson, 1990.

Picirilli, Robert E. *Grace, Faith, Free Will*. Nashville: Randall House, 2002.

_____. "Foreknowledge, Freedom, and the Future." *Journal of the Evangelical Theological Society* 43:2 (June 2000) 259-271.

Pinnock, Clark H. "Divine Election as Corporate, Open, and Vocational." *Perspectives on Election: Five Views*. Chad Owen Brand, ed. Nashville: Broadman & Holman, 2006.

Piper, John. *The Justification of God*. Grand Rapids: Baker, 1983. 2nd ed. Baker, 1993.

Plantinga, Alvin. *God, Freedom, and Evil*. Grand Rapids: Eerdmans, 1974.

Pope, William Burt. *A Compendium of Christian Theology*. 3 vols. London: Wesleyan Conference Office, 1880.

Powers, Daniel G. *New Beacon Bible Commentary: 1 & 2 Peter/Jude*. Kansas City: Beacon Hill, 2010.

Reasoner, Vic. *A Wesleyan Theology of Holy Living for the 21st Century*. 2 vols. Evansville, IN: Fundamental Wesleyan, 2012.

_____. *A Fundamental Wesleyan Commentary on Romans*. 2 vols. 2nd ed. Evansville, IN: Fundamental Wesleyan 2020.

Salmond, Steward Dingwall Fordyce. "Ephesians." *The Expositor's Greek Testament*. W. Robertson Nicoll, ed. 5 vols. 1897-1910. Reprint, Grand Rapids: Eerdmans, 1983.

Sanday, William and Arthur C. Headlam. *International Critical Commentary: A Critical and Exegetical Commentary on the Epistle to the Romans*. 1895. Reprint, Edinburgh: T&T Clark, 1950.

Schaeffer, Francis. *The Finished Work of Christ: The Truth of Romans 1-8*. Wheaton, IL: Crossway, 1998.

Schreiner, Thomas R. *Baker Exegetical Commentary on the New Testament: Romans*. Grand Rapids: Baker, 1998.

_____. *1-2 Peter, Jude*. Nashville: Broadman & Holman, 2003.

Schrenk, Gottlob. "ἐκλέγομαι." *Theological Dictionary of the New Testament*. Vol. 4. Gerhard Kittel, ed. Grand Rapids: Eerdmans, 1967.

Shank, Robert. *Elect in the Son*. Springfield, MO: Westcott, 1970.

Snodgrass, Klyne. *The NIV Application Commentary: Ephesians*. Grand Rapids: Zondervan, 1996.

Sproul, R. C. *Chosen by God*. Wheaton, IL: Tyndale, 1986.

_____. *The Gospel of God*. 1994. Reprint, Ross-shire, Scotland: Christian Focus, 1999.

_____. *Andrew's Expositional Commentary: 1-2 Peter*. Wheaton, IL: Crossway, 2011.

_____, ed. *The Reformation Study Bible*. Nashville: Thomas Nelson, 2001. Formerly titled *The New Geneva Study Bible* (1995).

Sproul, R. C. Jr. *Almighty Over All*. Grand Rapids: Baker, 1999.

Stanglin, Keith D. A and Thomas H. McCall, *Jacob Arminius: Theological of Grace*. New York: Oxford University Press, 2012.

Steele, Daniel. *Half-Hours with St. Paul*. 1894. Reprint, Salem, OH: Schmul, 1961.

Steele, David N. and Curtis C. Thomas. *Romans: An Interpretive Outline*. Phillipsburg, NJ: Presbyterian and Reformed, 1963.

Stott, John R. W. *God's New Society*. Downers Grove, IL: InterVarsity, 1979.

Summers, Thomas O. *The Epistle of Paul, the Apostle, to the Romans, in the Authorized Version; with a New Translation and Commentary*. Nashville: Southern Methodist Publishing House, 1881.

Sutcliffe, Joseph. *A Commentary on the Old and New Testaments*. 1834. Reprinted, Salem, OH: Allegheny, 1999.

Talbott, Thomas B. "Universal Reconciliation and the Inclusive Nature of Election." *Perspectives on Election: Five Views*. Chad Owen Brand, ed. Nashville: Broadman & Holman, 2006.

Thiessen, Henry. *Introductory Lectures in Systematic Theology*. Grand Rapids: Eerdmans, 1949.

Torrance, Thomas F. *Incarnation: The Person and Life of Christ*. Robert T. Walker, ed. Downers Grove, IL: InterVarsity, 2008.

_____. *Atonement: The Person and Work of Christ*. Robert T. Walker, ed. Downers Grove, IL: InterVarsity, 2009.

Tozer, A. W. *The Knowledge of the Holy*. New York: Harper & Row, 1961.

Vanderhoof, Wesley E. "Ephesians." *Asbury Bible Commentary*. Eugene E. Carpenter and Wayne McCown, eds. Grand Rapids: Zondervan, 1992.

Vincent, Marvin. *Word Studies in the New Testament*. 4 vols. 1887. Reprint, Grand Rapids: Eerdmans,1946.

Vincent of Lérins. *Commonitory*. *Nicene and Post Nicene Fathers*. Second Series. Vol. 11. Philip Schaff and Henry Wace, eds. Reprint, Grand Rapids: Eerdmans, 1978.

Wallace, Daniel B. *Greek Grammar Beyond the Basics: An Exegetical Syntax of the New Testament*. Grand Rapids: Zondervan, 1996.

Walls, Jerry L. "Can God Save Anyone He Will?" *Scottish Journal of Theology* 38 (1985) 155-172.

Wang, Joseph S. "Romans." *Asbury Bible Commentary*. Eugene E. Carpenter and Wayne McCown, eds. Grand Rapids: Zondervan, 1992.

Watson, Richard. *Theological Institutes*. 2 vols. 1823-1829. Reprint, New York: Hunt & Eaton, 1889.

_____. *A Biblical and Theological Dictionary*. New York: Carlton & Porter, 1832.

Wesley, John. *The Bicentennial Edition of the Works of John Wesley*. Frank Baker and Richard P. Heitzenrater, eds. 35 vols. when complete. Nashville: Abingdon, 1976-.

_____. *Explanatory Notes Upon the New Testament*. 1754.

Reprint, Salem, OH: Schmul, 1976.

_____. *The Works of the Rev. John Wesley*. Joseph Benson, ed. 17 vols. London: Thomas Cordeaux, 1812.

Whedon, Daniel D. *Commentary on the New Testament*. 5 vols. 1860-1880. Reprint, Salem, OH: Schmul, 1977-1978.

Wiley, H. Orton and Ross E. Price. *The Epistle to the Ephesians: A Commentary*. Salem, OH: Allegheny, 2004.

Williams, Colin. *John Wesley's Theology Today*. Nashville: Abingdon, 1960.

Wood, A. Skevington. "Ephesians." *The Expositor's Bible Commentary*. Vol. 11. Frank E. Gaebelein, ed. Grand Rapids: Zondervan, 1978.

Wright, R. K. McGregor. *No Place for Sovereignty*. Downers Grove, IL: InterVarsity, 1996.

Wynkoop, Mildred Bangs. *Foundations of Wesleyan-Arminian Theology*. Kansas City: Beacon Hill, 1967.

www.ingramcontent.com/pod-product-compliance
Lightning Source LLC
Chambersburg PA
CBHW060201050426
42446CB00013B/2940